Out of Religion & Into Relationship

Connecting With God Beyond The Church Walls

Xavier LeMond

LEMOND PUBLISHING

Out of Religion & Into Relationship:
Connecting With God Beyond The Church Walls

ISBN:
979-8-9994686-1-1(Paperback)
979-8-9994686-0-4 (eBook)

Contents

Author's Note

This book has been two decades in the making, though its foundations go back much further, woven into the fabric of my entire life. For the last 20 years, I've been jotting down notes, dreams, and inspirations – impressions that God has placed on my heart, moments when the Holy Spirit has spoken, and insights that might seem to arrive out of nowhere but clearly came from Him.

Consequently, a pen and notebook have rarely been far from reach wherever I've gone. Experience has taught me that God's voice doesn't always follow a schedule. The Holy Spirit speaks when He wills, often in the moments we least expect but most need. Over the years, I've collected countless words of knowledge, revelations, and glimpses into the heart of God – pieces of a puzzle I didn't have the clarity to arrange and compile.

Until now.

There is a divine order and timing to all things. The ancient Greek word for this is "Kairos," meaning "the right or critical moment." I refer to a God-appointed time when events align perfectly with His purpose. Writing this book was no exception. Though I struggled for a long time to bring these thoughts together in a clear, cohesive manner, I've come to realize that the timing wasn't about me. It was about you, dear reader. God prepared this message not just for me to share, but for you to receive.

And this moment, right here and right now, is the moment He intended for you to encounter it.

So, however, you've come across this book – whether by chance, recommendation, or perhaps even skepticism – it's no accident. God has been preparing you for these truths, just as He prepared me to write them.

I pray that as you read this, the Spirit of God will speak to your spirit, guide you, inspire you, and bless you abundantly. May these words ignite your faith, deepen your understanding, and draw you into the vibrant, transformative relationship with God that you were created to experience and participate in.

Introduction

For too many believers, "church" has become a place of frustration rather than fulfillment. Week after week, they attend services, try to engage and participate in programs, but walk away feeling oddly empty and discouraged.

If you've ever felt like this, if you've experienced the disillusionment that comes from discovering that the institution you trusted for spiritual growth has left you wounded, burned out, or spiritually stagnated, if you've invested your time, energy, and heart into church life, only to find yourself wondering, "Is this all there is?"

...You're not alone.

Countless others have wrestled with the same question, felt the sting of being judged or dismissed, and found themselves saddled with a burden of unrealistic expectations. They've walked a hollow routine of rituals that seem disconnected from the kind of vibrant faith they had hoped to have.

Many have walked away from church altogether, unable to reconcile the God they've longed for in their hearts with the rigid structures that often bear His name. Others remain, quietly struggling, looking for something deeper but unsure how to find it.

Chances are you've sensed that there must be more – more to faith, more to life, more to knowing God. I'm here to tell you that you're absolutely right. There *is* more. Much more.

No professed Christian should be living a life marked by powerlessness, frustration, anxiety, and a lingering sense of unfulfillment. But a great number of them do. Though they have accepted Christ and have the promise of salvation, the might and strength of God in their personal lives is small and distant. They believe but fail to fully grasp the magnitude of what Christ has accomplished for them, and they don't realize the blessings He has already provided to bring victory and purpose to their lives now, even as they await His return.

At the heart of their struggle is a misunderstanding or a lack of understanding about the Spirit-led life. Many believers have yet to recognize the importance of living by the Spirit of God, much less how to do so. They approach faith as a matter of obligation or ritual, rather than as a transformative journey fueled by a personal, intimate relationship with God. They miss out on the abundant life Christ promised because they rely on their own strength and understanding rather than allowing the Spirit to guide, empower, and sustain them.

Here is the truth that so many have yet to embrace: God has a life plan for you, a plan that satisfies your deepest desires and leads to an abundant, fulfilling life. This isn't some generic roadmap. It's not a one-size-fits-all approach. Because God knows you intimately (He knew you before you were born), His plan is uniquely tailored to your strengths, talents, and purpose. Within that divine plan, you find the true measure of success, not as the world defines it, but as it is defined by Heaven. You will find the fulfillment your heart has been longing for, both in this life and in the life to come.

But God doesn't just know you, He *claims* you. Personally. Individually. He called you by name and set His love upon you long before you ever heard of Him or turned your heart toward Him. He has been pursuing you with relentless love since before you were born, orchestrating every step of your journey to bring you closer to Him.

And His love for you is beyond comprehension. It is not conditional. It is not transactional. It is not based on anything you have done or could ever do. It simply *is*. God's love for you is infinite, eternal, and unshakable. And because of that love, He has a plan for your life that is so good, so profound, and so perfectly aligned with who you are that it exceeds anything you could ever imagine. It is more than enough. It will never leave you wanting.

So why, then, do so many Christians live outside of the fullness of Christ's promises? Why do they settle for mere survival when God has called them to thrive? These are questions that this book will answer in more detail, but the short answer is found in your direct relationship with God.

Your life is not supposed to be one of striving in your own strength, but abiding and resting in God's provision, listening for His voice, and walking in the purpose He has laid out for you. It is a life of abundance, fulfillment, and peace, not of your own efforts, but through the transformative work of the Spirit within you.

God is ready to equip you with His strength and to guide you every step of the way. What He asks is that you trust Him and allow His Spirit to move through you. When you do, you will discover a life so rich, so full of joy and purpose, that it will surpass anything you ever thought possible. Because that is who God is: A loving Father who withholds no good thing from His children.

That truth is hard for many people to believe for a myriad of reasons I'm about to explain. We've been poorly taught.

What if the rituals and routines you've been told are essential to faith were actually keeping you from experiencing the fullness of what God desires for your life? There is more to God than what most experience within the walls of institutionalized religion. What if the key to unlocking a vibrant, transformational relationship with Him has been within your reach all along?

This book is about discovering that key. It's about understanding the constraints of religion, finding your way past the barriers and obstacles that have held you back, moving beyond the limitations of institutionalized faith, and stepping into the boundless freedom and joy of a direct, personal relationship with Him.

You weren't created to live in the shadow of tradition or to measure your spiritual worth by how well you follow religious rules. God created you for divine intimacy — a dynamic, life-changing relationship that goes far beyond what most of us have been taught in church.

Through Christ, He has made Himself fully accessible to you, not through intermediaries, hierarchies, or man-made institutions, but through His Spirit, who lives in you. (See **Romans 8:9**)

I want to be clear that this book is not an attack on church. It's not about forsaking the community or rejecting the value of fellowship. But it *is* about putting church in its proper place as a tool for growth and encouragement rather than the foundation of your faith.

Most importantly, it is about helping you discover the God who desires to meet you where you are, who wants to speak directly to your heart, and who has a plan to transform your life from the inside out.

My prayer for you, as you read this book, is that you will come to understand the incredible freedom, love, and purpose that come from knowing God, not just personally but intimately. I want to give you the knowledge and the inspiration to break free from the weight of religious expectations. What you need is a conversational encounter with the One who has been pursuing you all along.

That means stepping boldly into the vibrant, dynamic relationship He designed you to have with Him; a relationship that leads to an exuberant life of joy, peace, and meaning.

I'm not talking about abandoning your faith. This is about reclaiming and realigning it properly. It's about stepping out of rituals or traditions and into relationship; cultivating a faith that honors God not just with your lips but with your heart, your mind, and your life.

What You Should Know About Me

Before we delve any deeper, I should tell you a bit about myself, my relationship with God, and what I believe is my God-given mission. I want to let you see how the principles I'll present have been woven into my own life story. My hope is that through understanding my background, you'll be encouraged to reflect on your own journey and be inspired to cultivate a deeper, direct connection with the God who desires to walk with you.

I was quite literally "attending church" before I was born. My mother was a devout churchgoer, attending services every week without fail, and while she was pregnant with me was no exception. This pattern continued throughout my childhood as I was raised in a fundamentalist church tradition. By the time I was old enough to read, I had already internalized most of the Bible stories. They weren't just tales to me – they were alive, vivid, and compelling. God wasn't some distant, abstract figure. He was someone I knew, someone I spoke to, even as a young child.

I was 5 years old when God revealed Himself to me as a loving Heavenly Father. Even at that young age, I somehow knew that He loved me – not in a conditional way tied to my behavior or actions, but with a love that simply *was*. I didn't earn it, and I couldn't lose it. His love wasn't based on whether I was a good or bad child. It was steadfast and unchanging, even when I made mistakes or did things that I knew wouldn't please Him.

Though I may not have fully understood the depth of it back then, I accepted His love in simple, child-like faith, and that truth became a foundational part of who I am.

There's a divine strength that comes from knowing you are loved; a strength that can't be replicated by anything else. It's not just a source of comfort or reassurance; it brings a genuine desire to do better and, more importantly, the power to *be* better. God's love doesn't just inspire change; it equips you for it.

For as long as I can remember, I've had a personal relationship with my Heavenly Father. Some might consider that unusual for a child, but I don't think it is. Children are naturally open, free from the cynicism, distractions, and wounds that adulthood tends to bring. What made my relationship with God unique wasn't that it began so early – it was that I never grew out of it.

As I grew older, that relationship didn't fade or get pushed aside by the demands of life. Instead, it deepened and matured, just as I did. My conversations with Him evolved from the simple, trusting prayers of a child into an ongoing, meaningful dialogue – a genuine relationship rooted in love and a desire to walk in alignment with His will.

But from my adolescence into my teenage years, something unsettling began to emerge. The God I knew intimately – the loving Heavenly Father I spoke to daily – was often not the God presented to me in church. In the denomination I grew up in, the Lord God Almighty was frequently portrayed as a stern taskmaster, a deity who demanded perfection and obedience to a long list of rules and rituals. He was someone you had to earn approval from, someone who was perpetually disappointed in your humanity.

This image clashed with the God that I knew as a loving Heavenly Father.

My Heavenly Father was not distant or unapproachable; He was loving, compassionate, and ever-present. The contrast between my personal experience with Him and what I was being taught in church created what I call a "religious schism" in my life. It wasn't a spiritual crisis – I never doubted God's existence or His love for me. Instead, it was a rebellion against the portrayal of God that I felt was inaccurate.

BECOMING A STUDENT OF THE SPIRIT

In my frustration, I turned to the only source I trusted implicitly: God Himself. I prayed a simple yet profound prayer, inviting the Holy Spirit to guide and teach me directly. *"Lord,"* I prayed, *"These things they are trying to teach seem ridiculous to me. I need You to show me who You really are and convict me of what You want me to know. If I need to believe it, it has to come through you. You have to convict me heart directly."*

I didn't realize it then, but I had echoed something similar to the words of David (the shepherd boy chosen by God to be the second king of Israel) with my request. In **Psalms 25:4-5** David wrote...

Show me your ways, O Lord, teach me your paths; guide me in your truth and teach me, for you are God my Savior, and my hope is in you all day long.

– Psalms 25:4-5

In doing so, I surrendered myself to the direct tutelage of the Spirit... just as Christ had promised us...

But the Counselor, the Holy Spirit, whom the Father will send in my name, will teach you all things and will remind you of everything I have said to you.

– John 14:26

At the time, I didn't fully grasp the significance of what I was asking, but God honored that prayer in ways I could never have anticipated.

From that moment on, I couldn't open the Scriptures without waves of depth and understanding of the Word as it applied to my life jumping out at me. It wasn't just intellectual comprehension; it was revelation. The Word of God became alive and real in a way that transcended anything I had experienced before. The Holy Spirit became my teacher, and the lessons He imparted weren't about theology per se – they were about life and how to live in alignment with the Kingdom of Heaven.

I learned from personal experience that the mysteries of God are only revealed through the power of the Holy Spirit and on His terms. He is exposed and discovered through faith, and only those in whom the Spirit abides can truly understand and accept them.

The Apostle Paul confirms this in the second chapter of **1 Corinthians**, starting in verse 9:

However, as it is written: "No eye has seen, no ear has heard, no mind has conceived what God has prepared for those who love him"-- but God has revealed it to us by his Spirit. The Spirit searches all things, even the deep things of God... We have not received the spirit of the world but the Spirit who is from God, that we may understand what God has freely given us. This is what we speak, not in words taught us by human wisdom but in words taught by the Spirit, expressing spiritual truths in spiritual words. The man without the Spirit does not accept the things that come from the Spirit of God, for they are foolishness to him, and he cannot understand them, because they are spiritually discerned.

– 1 Corinthians 2:9-10,12-14

A BROADER CALLING

The gift I received that day led me to serve in many roles within the church – Bible teacher, worship leader, ordained minister, and more. In the years that followed, I served in various denominations, each with its own traditions and doctrines. I went wherever God sent me, striving to share the insights and revelations I had received. For the longest time, I thought my life was to be about teaching biblical knowledge and those things I had come to understand in scripture.

But it was never about what I knew.

It was about something far deeper – helping others cultivate intimate relationships with God themselves. When it comes to the Lord and the nature of His Kingdom, it's your personal relationship with Him that makes the difference because knowledge also comes from God.

Divine wisdom and understanding, I've learned, are born out of intimacy with God. Knowledge doesn't transform people's lives; a divine relationship does.

In our churches, we've "intellectualized" things to the point that we believe it's all about getting the doctrine right. Big mistake. God isn't judging you by how well you "figure out" His Word. What He wants is for you to learn to recognize, listen to, trust His voice, and follow His direction.

I've spent decades learning what it really means to get personal with God, releasing my own expectations, and growing to the point where God needed me to be in order to fully embrace His purpose for me.

What took a long time to get through my thick skull was that because I was willing and opened my heart, the Holy Spirit instructed me despite all my inherent shortcomings and insufficiencies. He is in the business of transformation.

Eventually, I realized what was most important for me to share with others is the fact that each and every one of us was created to have a much closer relationship with the Father, Son, and Holy Spirit than we imagine.

My mission, I now see clearly, is to help believers – especially those who are wounded, disillusioned, or stuck in cycles of religious routine – break free from the constraints of institutions and step into the vibrant, transformative relationship with God that they were created to have.

Intimacy with God matters.

THE CALL OF THE EKKLESIA

Although I am one, I don't always refer to myself as "Christian," not because I don't identify with or am ashamed of the term, but because the noun has been so misused and abused by so many people and institutions. People have preconceived notions of what a Christian is and many who claim the title have little idea what it means. I understand completely why Gandi once said, **"I like your Christ, I do not like your Christians. Your Christians are so unlike your Christ." – Mahatma Gandhi**

Given the opportunity, I prefer to call myself an "Ekklesian," a term derived from the Greek word "Ekklesia," which is the word Jesus used to describe His followers.

When the Lord said to Simon Peter, *"**Upon this rock I will build my church...**"* in **Matthew 16:18**, the word He used wasn't "church" at all. It was "Ekklesia," literally translated as "the called-out ones." He wasn't talking about institutions, hierarchies, or buildings. Ekklesia denotes a people, a purpose, or an assembly convened for a particular purpose. Christ was referring to an assembly of people, each and every one uniquely gifted and called, united under the guidance of the Holy Spirit; a gathering of believers united in shared purpose, mutual love, and devotion to God.

Unfortunately, when King James commissioned the King James Version of the Bible, he mandated the use of the word "church" instead of "Ekklesia." This was a deliberate effort to support the hierarchical structure of the Church of England and reinforce his authority as king and the church's Supreme Governor, as he called himself. The result is that the true meaning Christ inferred of "Ekklesia" – a "called out," assembly with no earthly hierarchy – was obscured and demoted. Instead, we got "church," a term that has come to represent institutions, denominations, human authority structures, and buildings.

But Jesus' purpose wasn't to establish an institution; He came to gather a people. The Great Commission He gave us in **Matthew 28:18-20** was not to create converts to fill pews but to make disciples – followers who would be empowered by the Holy Spirit and led by Him to impact the world. This mission wasn't limited to clergy or religious professionals; it was, and is, a calling for **every** believer.

My good friend, **Jon Ashcraft**, sums the situation up concisely in his book, "Becoming A Second Mile Leader":

"Many Christians have either forgotten their assignments or have never been informed of our duty as believers.

"In most cases, our churches are filled with people who have never been taught what the Bible actually says regarding their role in the army of God. Most of this can be traced back to the state church being established in Rome. Until that time, the early church understood their responsibilities as believers. They were soldiers in God's army, assigned the task of advancing the kingdom of God against the gates of Hell. Jesus called the church the ekklesia – agents of change that would destroy Hell's government. Jesus knew Hell would stand no chance against people who understood that they are soldiers in the army of God when they are trained and willing to perform their duties."

– Jon Ashcraft, "Becoming A Second Mile Leader"

Simply put, the Ekklesia are otherwise "ordinary" people (think of the type of people Jesus surrounded himself with) whose passion, desire, and goal is to be one of the many that God can and does entrust with the world for the cause of Christ.

Far too many believers do not understand the purpose of their faith. They think that going to church and striving to be good satisfy what the Lord wants from them. They have little conception of God's true purpose for their lives.

Part I:

God & Man

LEMOND PUBLISHING

Chapter One

Children of A Greater God

In the beginning, humanity's connection to God was both a profound reality and a reflection of God's ultimate intent for us. Adam and Eve's existence was defined by a direct relationship with their Creator – a personal and deeply intimate communion. **Genesis 3:8** tells us that they walked and talked with God in the cool of the day, an image that paints a picture of perfect harmony and closeness.

They were not merely created beings; they were God's children, formed in His image and likeness (see **Genesis 1:27**) and imbued with His Spirit, designed to reflect His nature and live in continuous fellowship with Him.

This was God's original design. The connection they shared with God was not just a benefit of their existence – it was the very essence of who they were. Their identity as individuals and as a couple was inseparable from the Creator who lovingly formed them. Their purpose – to tend the earth, multiply, and extend the community of God – was an extension of this intimate relationship.

But when sin entered the picture, everything changed.

Sin, at its core, isn't merely about breaking rules; it's about breaking relationship. When Adam and Eve disobeyed God by eating from the Tree of the Knowledge of Good and Evil, they rejected their dependence on Him and chose another path to define good and evil for themselves. (See **Genesis 3:6**)

This was an act of defiance that severed their unique, spiritual connection with God.

The consequences were immediate and devastating. Before their sin, they had been naked and unashamed (**Genesis 2:25**), fully known and fully loved in the presence of their Creator. Afterward, they were overwhelmed by shame, hiding from God and covering themselves with fig leaves (**Genesis 3:7**). Their act of hiding was symbolic of their new reality: Separation from the God who had been their source of identity, security, and purpose.

This separation wasn't just a physical exile from Eden; it was a spiritual fracture that rippled through every aspect of their being. They were no longer whole. Their communion with God was broken, and this brokenness introduced fear, disgrace, guilt, and suffering into the human experience. Their relationship with each other was also affected, as blame and mistrust entered their dynamic (**Genesis 3:12-13**).

The once-perfect unity they had shared with God and with one another was shattered. But even in their sin, they were still fully known and fully loved by Him.

In this moment of devastation, God's redemptive plan for them and for humanity to follow was already unfolding. While sin brought about separation, it did not extinguish God's love or His intent to restore the connection that had been lost.

In **Genesis 3:15**, sometimes referred to as the protoevangelium or "first gospel," God promised that Eve's offspring would crush the head of the serpent, foreshadowing the coming of Christ, who would ultimately defeat sin and death.

Throughout the Old Testament, we see the seeds of God's redemptive plan woven into the narrative of His people. Although the direct connection between humanity and God had been disrupted, God never stopped pursuing His creation. He established covenants with individuals like Noah, Abraham, and Moses, creating ways for His people to draw nearer to Him, even in their fallen, sinful state.

The tabernacle and later the temple served as physical representations of God's presence among His people, tangible reminders of His willingness to dwell with them despite their sin.

Yet Israel's covenants with God were predicated on works and rituals – laws and sacrifices that they repeatedly proved incapable of keeping fully. The sacrificial system, while providing a temporary means of atonement for sin, highlighted their inability to achieve righteousness on their own and ultimately pointed forward to the perfect and final sacrifice of Jesus Christ. Even in the midst of their rebellion and failure to uphold their covenant, God's love remained steadfast, and His plan for restoration continued to unfold.

Through the prophets, He persistently reminded Israel of His desire for relationship, calling them to return to Him with their whole hearts, promising restoration and hope to those who would seek Him. (See **Jeremiah 29:13, Joel 2:12-13**)

The death of Christ on the cross marked the fulfillment of God's redemptive plan. Jesus paid the price of sin for all men and restored what had been lost. He bridged the gap that sin had created and made it possible for those who were willing to have a direct, personal relationship with God again.

This is the essence of the New Covenant – a covenant not based on external rituals or sacrifices that we perform, but on what Christ did for us and the transformative work of the Holy Spirit operating within us.

Whereas the Old Covenant required priests to serve as intermediaries between God and His people, the New Covenant allows every believer to approach God directly. As **Hebrews 10:19-22** beautifully explains, we can now *"draw near to God with a sincere heart and with the full assurance that faith brings"* because of the sacrifice of Jesus. The Holy Spirit dwells within us, testifying to our identity as children of God and enabling us to live in communion with Him. (See **Romans 8:15-16**).

But even with the restoration of this divine connection, humanity still grapples with the effects of sin. The spiritual, emotional, and relational consequences of separation from God are deeply ingrained in our fallen nature. Many believers continue to feel distant from God, burdened by guilt, shame, or the weight of religious expectations.

The question is, "Why?"

We'll begin to answer that in the next chapter.

For now, the good news is that the longing for connection with God is evidence of His Spirit at work within you. As **Ecclesiastes 3:11** reminds us, God has *"set eternity in the human heart."* This innate desire for something beyond yourself points back to the Creator who made you for relationship with Him.

Living in alignment with God's original design requires you to recognize and embrace the counterintuitive truth that you are not made whole through your own efforts but through the transforming power of the Holy Spirit at work within you. This means surrendering your brokenness to Him and allowing His love to heal, restore, and mature you. It's a matter of trust. It also means seeking Him not out of obligation but out of a genuine desire to know and be known by Him.

The invitation is clear: As a believer, God is calling you back into the perfect community He intended from the beginning. Through Jesus, the way has been made, and through the Holy Spirit you are empowered. The question is, will you respond? Will you allow Him to restore the connection that sin disrupted and lead you into the abundant life He created you to live?

God's intent has always been to dwell with His people, to walk and talk with us just as He did before the Fall. This is the heart of the gospel — not just salvation from sin but restoration to relationship. It is a call to return to your true spiritual identity as His child, to live in the fullness of His love, and to extend that love to others.

As children of God, we are no longer distant observers, on the outside looking in, hoping for access to His presence. Through Christ, we've been invited into a direct, intimate relationship with Him, able to experience His love, hear His voice, and be led by His Spirit. Under the New Covenant, we are offered a life of freedom and closeness – a relationship with God that allows us to discover and explore our spiritual identity and live out His purpose for us without the weight of guilt or religious dogma that so many of us have been exposed to.

This relationship represents a new and different kind of engagement, not one based on rules and rituals but on the Spirit of God abiding within. Christ's purpose wasn't just to save us but to restore a vibrant, living connection between humanity and God. He opened a path to a relationship built on love, grace, and spiritual intimacy; one that empowers us to walk in step with Him... every day.

If nothing else, it is very important that you understand salvation is the beginning of your divine journey, not the end goal or reward for any achievement on your part. From that point, once you've accepted salvation and been saved, it is the Holy Spirit of God who molds you into who you were created to be and shapes you toward perfection. You are on the "potter's wheel," as it were, in the Master's hands. Your spiritual growth is not about striving to become a "better person," it's about surrendering to the transformation process that the Spirit desires to work within you.

And it's a process that takes time.

You are not just another soul wandering through life; you are the deliberate creation of a loving Father who has called you His own. If you could see yourself the way God sees you, your life would never be the same.

The journey back to God's original design is not without challenges, but it is one of unparalleled joy, peace, and purpose. When you step into a properly restored relationship with God, the process of becoming who and what you were meant to be – a reflection of His glory, a vessel of His grace, and an empowered son or daughter of God – that is when the process begins.

That is how you achieve the fullness of who you were created to be.

Chapter Two

Seeing God Beyond Our Misperceptions

I understand that for some, the idea of being intimate with God or getting to know Him on a deeper, far more personal level can feel overwhelming, even frightening. There is a natural, human response that arises when we find ourselves in the presence of the Almighty: An acute awareness of our own shortcomings – our inadequacy, unworthiness, and insufficiency. This realization can be paralyzing, and for many, it perpetuates a distorted view of God that is far from His true nature.

Even among believers who should know better, misleading suppositions persist. Too often, God is presented as little more than a stern, distant figure, an old man on a throne who:

- Is impossible to please

- Is on the constant watch for our failures

- Is eager to condemn.

- Is perpetually angry and dissatisfied with our performance, no matter how much we try.

But God is not Zeus. He's not waiting to throw lightning bolts at you or dispense corporal punishment for your indiscretions.

Others just mistakenly think of God as someone who is indifferent to their plight and far less interested in the details of their lives than in seeing if they measure up.

Misperceptions like these are not only inaccurate – they are outright falsehoods and lies, distortions of God's character built on human fear, limited understanding, and centuries of poor religious tradition.

God already knows your every failing and shortcoming. He's not waiting for you to get yourself together on your own because, frankly, He knows you can't, and He doesn't expect you to.

Humanity has always struggled to grasp the nature of the divine. In our imperfect comprehension, we attempt to "create" God in our own image. Throughout history, mankind has fashioned gods of wood, stone, and imagination — gods who reflect our flawed understanding of divine power, justice, and control. Even as Christian believers, we can fall into this trap, projecting our fears, doubts, and human expectations onto God. We seek to confine Him to a framework we can comprehend, shaping Him into someone who aligns with our finite view of how things "should" be.

But here is the issue: Our natural perception of God is inherently flawed. And because of this, we risk missing the truth of who He is and what He desires for us.

When you align yourself with the Spirit of God and surrender to His divine wisdom, your limited perspective is replaced with heavenly insight. The Spirit opens your eyes to Truth that cannot be perceived "in the natural." You begin to see not only God's immeasurable glory but also His boundless love and complete acceptance of you, just as you are. And in that love, He gently raises you to greater heights.

You come to understand that God is not looking for perfection. He is not waiting to condemn you or tally your failures. Instead, He is actively working within you, transforming you from the inside out. As you grow in spiritual awareness, you realize that any righteousness you achieve is not your own doing but the work of God within you. He makes you perfect... in Him.

It is His Spirit – alive and active in you – that elevates you to His higher standard, enabling you to live a life that reflects His heart. His love and acceptance are not earned; they are freely given. And through His Spirit, He accomplishes what you never could on your own.

This is the God we serve. Not distant. Not angry. Not unreachable. But a loving Father who draws you closer to Him, heals your wounds, and shapes you into the person He created you to be.

The Nature of An Infinite God

By His grace, I've come to understand that the fullness of God's mysteries can only be revealed by the power of the Holy Spirit, and only on His terms. God is not discovered through mere human deduction or intellectual pursuit; He makes Himself known to those who seek Him, but true comprehension and acceptance of the divine truths of His nature is only possible through the faith that He provides and by the abiding presence of His Spirit within us.

As Paul wrote in **1 Corinthians**, chapter 2:

"No eye has seen, no ear has heard, no mind has conceived what God has prepared for those who love him"-- but God has revealed it to us by his Spirit. The Spirit searches all things, even the deep things of God... We have not received the spirit of the world but

the Spirit who is from God, that we may understand what God has freely given us. This is what we speak, not in words taught us by human wisdom but in words taught by the Spirit, expressing spiritual truths in spiritual words. The man without the Spirit does not accept the things that come from the Spirit of God, for they are foolishness to him, and he cannot understand them, because they are spiritually discerned.

— 1 Corinthians 2:9-10, 12-14

God's vastness and the fullness of His goodness simply cannot be discerned through casual observation or mere human understanding. Yet, in His great love and mercy, He has made Himself known in ways that even the simplest of hearts can comprehend. He is revealed in in the world around us, leaving no one without a witness of His glory and power.

Romans 1:19-20 confirms this:

"...since what may be known about God is plain to them, because God has made it plain to them. For since the creation of the world God's invisible qualities – his eternal power and divine nature – have been clearly seen, being understood from what has been made, so that people are without excuse..."

— Romans 1:20

When Moses asked God who He was, God revealed Himself as *"I Am"* (**Exodus 3:13-14**). This declaration transcends time and space, revealing an ever-present, eternal God who defies human understanding.

God is the Creator of all that is. He is the Alpha and the Omega (**Revelation 1:8**) – the Self-existent, Self-sustaining One. He did not come from something else, and there is nothing outside of Him that gave Him His being. By Him, through Him, and with Him, the universe exists and is held together. Simply stated, apart from God, nothing could exist – not even time itself.

As creatures bound by time, this truth is difficult to fully comprehend. Everything we experience is constrained by time: Our births, our deaths, and every moment in between. Time is the framework through which we view our entire existence. Yet God is not constrained by time, for time itself is His creation. He existed before the beginning of all things and will continue long after this world has passed away. He is not "before" or "after" as we understand it – He simply *is*.

God the Almighty is omnipotent, omniscient, and omnipresent. He is all-powerful, all-knowing, and ever-present, existing everywhere and in all things at all times. Obtaining a glimpse of this reality is critical for understanding the nature of sin and its profound consequences.

But first, let me expand just a bit on these 3 aspects of God:

God is omnipotent; He is all-powerful. By His will and word, all things came into being and continue to exist. From the complexity of human life down to the smallest pebble by a nameless stream, everything is sustained by Him. He is the source of all life and the Creator of everything seen and unseen. From the vast cosmos to the smallest atom, every part of creation testifies to His power and creative design. And yet, He is not limited to His creation. God exists outside and beyond all that we can perceive.

As **Isaiah 40:25-26** so beautifully says:

"To whom will you compare me? Or who is my equal?" says the Holy One. Lift your eyes and look to the heavens: Who created all

these? He who brings out the starry host one by one, and calls them each by name. Because of His great power and mighty strength, not one of them is missing."

— Isaiah 40:25-26

God is omniscient. He knows all things, from the beginning of time to the end of eternity. Nothing escapes His sight, and His plans are perfect and complete. He is intimately aware of every detail of His creation, from the grandest galaxies to the smallest thoughts of your heart.

"Nothing in all creation is hidden from God's sight. Everything is uncovered and laid bare before the eyes of him to whom we must give account."

— Hebrews 4:13

"From one man he made all the nations, that they should inhabit the whole earth; and he marked out their appointed times in history and the boundaries of their lands."

— Acts 17:26

And God is omnipresent. He is everywhere at all times. There is no place where He is not, and there is nothing that exists apart from Him. There is no corner of creation where He is not present. His glory and presence fill all of creation, sustaining it by His will and power. There is no place where you can escape His reach, no depth too deep, no height too high.

"Where can I go from your Spirit? Where can I flee from your presence? If I go up to the heavens, you are there; if I make my bed

in the depths, you are there. If I rise on the wings of the dawn, if I settle on the far side of the sea, even there your hand will guide me, your right hand will hold me fast."

– Psalm 139:7-10

God is not confined to a specific location in the stars or galaxies. His dwelling place is not limited to heaven or some far-off, incomprehensible realm. God's presence is infinite and ubiquitous. He is here, there, and everywhere at the same time. It is by His sustaining presence that the heavens, the stars, and the earth are held together, and apart from His presence, all things would cease to exist.

As the apostle Paul writes:

"He is before all things, and in Him all things hold together"

– Colossians 1:17

It is this truth that helps us understand why sin inevitably leads to death. (See **Romans 6:23**) The death brought about by sin is not merely physical death, what Jesus often referred to as sleep. The ultimate consequence of sin is the second death: The permanent, irrevocable separation from God, which results in the death of the soul and the end of existence. This is the eternal separation, a fate far more devastating than any earthly death.

I will take flak for saying this, but this isn't a moral issue – it is a law of existence. Apart from God, there is no life, no being, no subsistence. Sin separates us from God, and separation from God truly is death.

Yet, above all of His divine characteristics, God is Love. Though His power and majesty may be incomprehensible, God is not distant or detached. He seeks to be deeply personal and profoundly engaged with each one of us.

And it is this love that many find the hardest to comprehend. His love is not like the conditional, fleeting love we typically experience in this world. It is the essence of His being and the foundation of all His actions. God's love is constant, unchanging, unshakeable, infinite, and unconditional.

He loved humanity before the fall, and His love remained steadfast even after sin entered the picture. It was out of this unrelenting love that He gave His only Son to redeem you, to pay the ultimate price for your transgressions, and to restore you to Himself.

God's love remains constant despite humanity's rebellion. It was in love that God the Father sent His Son to redeem us. It was in love that Jesus willingly endured the cross to reconcile us to the Father. And it is in love that the Holy Spirit dwells within us, guiding, comforting, and transforming us. **Romans 5:8** tells us:

"But God demonstrates his own love for us in this: While we were still sinners, Christ died for us."

– Romans 5:8

God knows you, loves you, and desires a relationship with you beyond anything you can imagine. But one thing blocks your perception of this incredible love and connection – *sin.*

Sin separates us from God, not because He withdraws His love, but because it blinds us to the truth of who He is. It distorts our understanding, making us doubt His goodness, His presence, and His intentions. Yet even in this, God provides a way back to Him through Jesus Christ. He made a way for us to overcome sin, to be restored to intimacy with Him, and to step into the fullness of His love and purpose for our lives.

The most basic truth of the universe is this: **God is**. And this truth changes everything. It is not a distant, abstract concept but a life-altering revelation that invites you into alignment with your Creator. As you embrace this truth, you will begin to see not only who God is but also who you are in Him. You will find your purpose, your identity, and your destiny. Because God is. And because He loves you.

Always.

This is our God – immeasurable, infinite, and uncontainable. Yet, He invites us into relationship with Him. He offers Himself to us not as a distant deity but as a loving Father, a Savior, and a constant Companion. His love is the foundation of all that we are and all that we are called to be. And it is through His Spirit that we are empowered to know Him, to walk with Him, and to reflect His love to the world.

Fortunately, God is not confined to our limited understanding. He makes Himself known to those who seek Him. And when we align our hearts with His, we begin to see beyond the natural and step into the fullness of who He is and who He created us to be. That is the beauty and wonder of knowing God – a journey that will never end but only grow deeper and richer as we walk with Him.

Chapter Three

What You Don't Know About Sin

J ust to recap: It is by God's sustaining presence that the heavens, the stars, and the earth are held together. Apart from His presence, all things would cease to exist.

Understanding this reality is critical for grasping the nature of sin and its profound consequences.

It is this reality that helps us understand why sin inevitably leads to death (See **Romans 6:23**). The death brought about by sin is not merely physical death or sleep. The ultimate consequence of sin is what some refer to as the second death: The permanent, irrevocable separation from God, which results in the death of the soul and the end of existence. This is eternal separation, a fate far more devastating than any earthly passing.

As Jesus warns:

"Do not be afraid of those who kill the body but cannot kill the soul. Rather, be afraid of the one who can destroy both soul and body in hell."

– Matthew 10:28

Sin entered this world through Adam and Eve, but its roots run deeper than their disobedience. Sin is far more than that, and it is imprudent to reduce it to a mere issue of moral failure. Sin is a greater issue than morality alone; it is separation from God – it is *anything* that comes between you and God; anything you prioritize over Him. Sin is the rejection of God, and apart from God, there is no existence.

This is something not always understood, even by other created beings. Until the resurrection of Christ, even Satan, the adversary of God, failed to comprehend the full significance of separation from his Creator. At the moment Jesus died on the cross, Satan believed he had achieved the ultimate victory. What he failed to realize was that his actions revealed to all the rest of Creation the depth of his deception and his defeat.

Before his rebellion, Satan was known as Lucifer, the brightest and most magnificent of all created beings. He was so impressive that he was called the *"son of the morning"*. (See **Isaiah 14:12**) As a pinnacle of God's creation, Lucifer was adorned with beauty and splendor almost beyond our ability to imagine. He is described in **Ezekiel 28:12-17**:

"You were the seal of perfection, full of wisdom and perfect in beauty. You were in Eden, the garden of God; every precious stone adorned you... You were anointed as a guardian cherub, for so I ordained you. You were on the holy mount of God... You were blameless in your ways from the day you were created till wickedness was found in you... Your heart became proud on account of your beauty, and you corrupted your wisdom because of your splendor. So I threw you to the earth..."

– Ezekiel 28:12-17

Lucifer was the highest of all created beings. But ultimately, he chose to reject his Lord and Creator. At some point, in his pride, he persuaded himself that he no longer had any need or love for God. He looked at the magnificence God had bestowed upon him and convinced himself that he was equal. He allowed a thought to take root:

"I will ascend above the heights of the clouds; I will make myself like the Most High"

– Isaiah 14:14

In his arrogance, Lucifer rejected God.

This was the origin of sin.

But why would God allow any created being to turn against Him? The answer lies in one of the greatest gifts God has given to us: Free will. God is love, and love cannot be forced – it must be freely given and freely received. Without the power to choose, love is meaningless. God did not create robots programmed to obey; He created beings capable of experiencing the fullness of His love and reflecting it back to Him... and to Creation.

The most important thing that God gives to all intelligent, created beings is free will – the power to choose. He wants your love in relationship with Him, but love cannot ever be forced. True love is given and chosen willingly.

Lucifer chose not to. He persuaded himself that he no longer needed God. This is what corrupted his understanding. He convinced himself, "God is holding me back. God doesn't love me. I can be my own god." In his rebellion, Lucifer became the *"father of lies"* (**John 8:44**), spreading his deceit to others.

A third of the angels in Heaven believed Lucifer's lies, sided with him, and chose to reject God themselves. (See **Revelation 12:4**) It was a rebellion rooted in a fundamental misunderstanding of who God is: Not only the Creator, but also the Sustainer of all that is. Everything that exists does so because of God's will and presence. Apart from Him, there is nothing.

The rebellion in Heaven was also a clash of ideas and beliefs: Trust versus distrust, love versus pride, truth versus deception. I believe that until then, all of creation had lived in perfect harmony with God's will. But the rebellion introduced doubt, jealousy, and unbelief. For the first time, created beings questioned the motives of their Creator.

Satan would have the world, indeed all of Creation, believe that he is God's equal, that good and evil are two opposing forces of comparable power. But this is another of his lies. The enemy is not in any way God's equal. He is a created being, subject to God's authority and bound by the limitations of his nature. As Paul reminds us about God:

"For by Him all things were created: things in heaven and on earth, visible and invisible, whether thrones or powers or rulers or authorities; all things were created by Him and for Him."

– Colossians 1:16

The enemy's falsehoods and misrepresentations have been perpetuated through the ages, designed to keep God's children from understanding the depth of His love and the truth of His character. But our Heavenly Father's love is unyielding. He has allowed the rebellion to continue for a time, not because He lacked the power to end it, but because He desires to reveal the fullness of His love and justice.

God's response to the rebellion and humanity's fall was not immediate destruction but divine patience. He has allowed the conflict to unfold so that all Creation can see the truth of His character, the result of sin, and the consequences of separation from Him.

It is for the enemy and his rebellious cohorts, just as Nahum prophesied to the people of Nineveh:

"Whatever you plot against the LORD, He will bring to an end. Affliction will not rise up a second time."

– Nahum 1:9

Throughout the history of the universe, through Christ's life, death, and resurrection, through Pentecost (namely the sending of the Holy Spirit), and through so much more, God demonstrates the lengths He goes to redeem His children. His love is incomprehensible, His patience unfathomable, and His justice perfect. He invites you to choose Him, to reject the lies of the enemy, and to walk in the truth of His love. For in Him, and only in Him, will you find abundant life, purpose, and eternal joy.

We'll discover why in the next chapter.

Chapter Four

A Reach Beyond Sin

God loves you.

These three words are the most transformative words you will ever hear in your lifetime. Yet, the love of God is so immense and so beyond measure that even those who believe in Him and have accepted the gift of salvation often struggle to grasp its depth.

We wonder: How can God truly love me? Especially when He knows the things I've done? How could He love someone like me, with all my flaws and failures?

These questions are akin to the words of King David thousands of years ago:

"What is man that you are mindful of him, the son of man that you care for him?"

— Psalm 8:4

What are we to God that He would even consider us? How is it possible that the Almighty, Creator of the universe, would concern Himself with our lives and circumstances?

As believers, we accept that God loves us beyond our comprehension. Otherwise, why would He send His Son to redeem us? Is there something about mankind that makes us special to Him?

Indeed, there is.

The key to understanding this is found in our origin. Genesis chapter 1 tells us:

"Then God said, 'Let us make man in our image, in our likeness.' So God created man in His own image, in the image of God He created them; male and female He created them."

— Genesis 1:26,27

Unlike anything else in creation that had come before, mankind was uniquely made in the very image of God. We are His masterpiece, created with intention, love, and purpose. In us, God did something unprecedented: He made beings not only *"fearfully and wonderfully made"* (**Psalm 139:14**) but fashioned to reflect His likeness; beings who were capable of direct fellowship with Him; His children, His progeny.

We were formed with three dimensions — body, soul, and spirit — reflecting the triune nature of God Himself. He endowed us with reasoning, imagination, and creative ability. He gave us the extraordinary gift of free will, the ability to choose, and the capacity to love.

You are more than your physical body, more than your talents or flaws, more than your past or present. God saw the complete, redeemed, and perfected version of you long before you took your first breath. He knows everything about you: Your strengths and weaknesses, your victories and failures... and He loves you fully and unconditionally.

My friend, God did not create you out of indifference or disinterest. He formed you with passionate love and a desire for a relationship with you. You were brought into existence to be part of His divine family, to participate in and share the love that flows eternally between the Father, the Son, and the Holy Spirit.

You are a child of the Most High God, lovingly known by Him before you were born, and far more important to Him than you may have ever realized. You are very much His child and He holds you in higher esteem than you hold yourself.

Although we were created from the dust of the earth, God's plan for us goes far beyond our earthly nature. He designed mankind to be more than mere physical beings. He made us living vessels, temples of His Spirit, meant to carry His own presence within us. (See **2 Corinthians 4:7**). God's desire is to abide in us and through us, transforming us from earthen vessels into reflections of His glory.

That's why the relationship He desires to have with you is deeply personal and intimate. His vision for your life has not wavered in the face of sin, despite any poor choices you've made, mistakes, or accusations of the enemy. God loves you with a passion that transcends time, and what He wants for you has never altered from the beginning.

I tell you again, God's love is not conditional. It is not based on your good deeds, your failures, or anything you have or have not done. It is constant, unchanging, and unrelenting.

So, why does the reality of God's love feel distant or hidden at times? The answer lies in the fall of man.

Adam and Eve began their lives in a perfect relationship with God. They walked with Him, talked with Him, and experienced His divine presence firsthand. They were stewards of the earth, enjoying the blessings of creation and the fullness of God's love. They lived in complete harmony with their Creator, unable to conceive anything of separation from Him.

But that possibility existed because God inherently allowed for choice. Remember, true love cannot exist without free will. So He endowed humanity with the power to choose Him or reject Him.

Tragically, they chose the latter.

The enemy, in the form of a serpent, tempted them with the same lies he had used to entice a third of heaven's angels. He whispered half-truths and subtle deceptions, implying that God was withholding something from them, that they could be more apart from Him than with Him. He implied that God had not been completely truthful, and that there was more to be gained apart from him than in obedience to him.

These same strategies remain in his arsenal of deception today. He contends that God is not fair or faithful or even real. Whatever the argument, the bottom line is to deceive as many as possible into believing that they do not need God.

This is what the world believes: That it has little or no use for the one true God. At best, the Enemy provides a distorted mockery of the Almighty. He offers a multitude of substitutions or false gods fashioned in warped images of our Heavenly Father. At worst, the world denies and ridicules His existence, disparaging and even seeking death for those who put their trust in His true self.

In Eden, as now, there had to be choice. Ultimately, every person has to make a conscious decision as to whether he or she is going to believe, trust, and follow the Creator... or not.

The first humans chose not to obey. Eve was beguiled by the Enemy in the form of a smooth-talking serpent, and Adam, though not deceived, chose Eve over God.

That's how sin found its way into our world. Their disobedience stained every human being who came after... with sin condemning all to its severe consequences.

When they disobeyed, sin entered the world. Their decision had far-reaching consequences, not just for themselves but for all of humanity. Sin brought shame, guilt, and separation from God. It introduced fear and self-condemnation, distorting their understanding of the Creator's love and their identity as His children.

Their failure was about more than disobedience, however. In their rebellion, they did gain knowledge of good and evil, learning from bitter personal experience what was right and what was wrong. They learned the painful difference between truth and falsehood firsthand. But it was a knowledge that came at so great a cost they couldn't even begin to imagine the consequences.

With that knowledge also came many awful things they didn't anticipate, not the least of which was self-condemnation and guilt. Sin gave access to something devastatingly detrimental: The accusing voice of the Enemy.

The Bible tells us in **Revelation 12:10** that Satan is the *"accuser of the brethren."* He wasted no time reminding Adam and Eve of their failure. Before God even confronted them, they judged themselves. They felt unworthy, ashamed, and exposed, and hid themselves from God. This was a marked contrast to the relationship they had previously enjoyed with Him. **Genesis 3:7–10** (NIV) lays it out for us:

"Then the eyes of both of them were opened, and they realized they were naked; so they sewed fig leaves together and made coverings for themselves. Then the man and his wife heard the sound of the Lord God as He was walking in the garden in the cool of the day, and they

hid from the Lord God among the trees of the garden. But the Lord God called to the man, 'Where are you?' He answered, 'I heard you in the garden, and I was afraid because I was naked; so I hid.'"

– Genesis 3:7-10

Sin distorted their perception of God. Where once they knew Him as loving and approachable, they now saw Him as a source of fear and judgment. This distortion, a result of sin that severed their connection to Him, also impaired their ability to sense and receive His love.

It continues to do the same for many today.

Through their disobedience, Adam and Eve gained the knowledge of good and evil, but at an excruciating cost. They lost their innocence, their peace, and their direct connection with God. We all became vulnerable to the accusing voice of an enemy who continually reminds humanity of its failures and unworthiness.

Although they recognized their own unworthiness, for they had disobeyed God, what they couldn't understand in their sin (and what we as sinful beings have trouble comprehending today) is God's ability and willingness to reach out beyond it. Sin had enslaved and separated them from their Heavenly Father. They unwittingly exchanged the truth of God and their relationship with Him for separation and distance, giving place to the Enemy's lies and constant accusations.

Through the failure of disobedience, every subsequent generation of humanity gained a certain knowledge of good and evil. But knowledge without the insight to use it properly is a curse. What had been lost was divine wisdom. And knowledge without wisdom was as destructive a thing then as it is in our world today.

We live in a world where knowledge is easy to come by. The Internet has made access to information – and disinformation, for that matter –

ubiquitous. But having knowledge and knowing what to do with that knowledge are two different things entirely.

Sin didn't change God's love for us. What it did was it obscure our ability to perceive and receive His love. This was the enemy's goal: To create a barrier between humanity and our Creator, to keep us from knowing and trusting in our Heavenly Father's unchanging love.

As humanity fell, so did our ability to discern truth from lies, good from evil, and so much more. Sin clouds our judgment and blinds us to the truth of our Heavenly Father's love and provision. The enemy tries to block our comprehension of God's ability and desire to reach beyond the sin that separates us from Him. Satan's lies ensnare us and keep us apart and unaware of God's true love and provision for us.

This is the first and foremost casualty of sin.

Although the fall of mankind was devastating for us, it did not take God by surprise. He prepared in advance to send a Savior – His Son, Christ Jesus – to bridge the chasm that sin had created between us and Himself.

God's love for you has never changed. The only thing that changed after the Fall was humanity's *perception* of Him. And that's the Enemy's greatest weapon – keeping you from seeing how deeply loved and wanted you are.

Through Christ, God demonstrated His desire and ability to reach beyond sin. He made a way for you to be reconciled to Him, to walk in a restored relationship, and to experience the fullness of His love once again.

God's love is relentless, His grace is sufficient, and His plan of redemption is perfect. All you need to do is accept it. For in Him, there is no condemnation, only love that reaches beyond sin to cleanse, restore, and redeem. He desires to transform and make you new.

Chapter Five

Redeemed and Restored

When Adam and Eve succumbed to sin, the consequences rippled through all of humanity to follow. Every man, woman, and child has been affected and tainted by their disobedience. In that moment, it seemed that all our fates were to be estranged from God.

But no.

God conceived and created us in love; His acts on our behalf are not afterthoughts. His love would not be defeated. Our Heavenly Father had a plan.

It was a supernatural plan, one beyond the comprehension of any created being. A divine plan that not only reconciles us to God but elevates us to unimaginable heights, crowning each of His children in glory and granting them the adoption into His eternal family.

Out of a love so deep that we can scarcely fathom it, the Son of God Himself would pay the price of sin for us. On our behalf, He would willingly endure death – *separation from His Father* – so that we might live, offering us the gift of salvation and adoption into the family of God.

And this gift would be freely given to all who accept it. God will not force it upon anyone. **John 3:17–18** tells us:

"For God did not send His Son into the world to condemn the world, but to save the world through Him. Whoever believes in Him is not condemned, but whoever does not believe stands condemned already because they have not believed in the name of God's one and only Son."

— John 3:17-18

"For as in Adam all die, so in Christ all will be made alive."
— 1 Corinthians 15:22

Through Adam's disobedience, all were corrupted by sin and separated from God. But through Christ's obedience and sacrifice, those who believe are restored to their Heavenly Father and granted eternal life. Only God could pay the price of sin for you, that you might live, and only through Him could death be defeated. This was the glorious plan that had been prepared from the beginning and it remains the foundation of our faith today.

"Yet to all who did receive Him, to those who believed in His name, He gave the right to become children of God – children born not of natural descent, nor of human decision or a husband's will, but born of God."

— John 1:12–13

When you receive Christ, you are not only saved but also adopted into the family of God. Being a son or daughter of God is not a perfunctory title – it is a profound and eternal reality. Through your faith in Christ, you become an adopted child of the Most High, a member of the royal Heavenly family.

This adoption carries with it both privilege and purpose. God chose you, not as an afterthought or by accident, but with intention and love. Long before you were born, He saw you, knew you, and planned for your redemption. And He did so for a greater purpose than just saving you from sin. He has called you to be a living testament to His love and redemption, not only for mankind but for all of Creation.

Worthiness Not Required

When you accepted the gift of salvation through Christ, you were re-deemed and reconciled to God. But this gift is just the beginning of your journey. Salvation is not the ultimate goal – it is the foundation upon which God will build the fullness of your destiny.

Let me repeat that: Salvation is not the finish line, it is the starting block. That's why the Lord doesn't care about where you've come from or what you've done. It doesn't matter. When you release sin to Him, it's forgiven. And forgotten.

The fact is, we have a much bigger time forgiving ourselves than God has forgiving us.

For some, life has been a series of failures, bad decisions, and brokenness. You're ashamed of your past, wrestling with your present, and feel unwor-thy. You're unsure of your place in His kingdom. But let me assure you: God's love for you is not dependent on your worthiness.

Not one of us is worthy in and of ourselves. Our best efforts, even from we might consider to be of great faith and accomplishment, when

compared to God's righteousness, fall woefully short. As it is written in
Isaiah 64:6:

*"All of us have become like one who is unclean, and all our
righteous acts are like filthy rags; we all shrivel up like a leaf, and
like the wind our sins sweep us away."*

– Isaiah 64:6

Every one of us *"...has sinned and fallen short of the glory of God."*
(See **Romans 3:23**) Yet, out of His abundant mercy and love, God extends
His grace to us. We are saved not by our works but by His grace through
our faith in Christ. The good works we do are the result of God's work in
us, not our own works or actions.

We cannot take credit for any of it, for it is all His doing. In **Ephesians
2:4—9** we read:

*"But because of His great love for us, God, who is rich in mercy,
made us alive with Christ even when we were dead in transgressions
– it is by grace you have been saved. And God raised us up with
Christ and seated us with Him in the heavenly realms in Christ
Jesus, in order that in the coming ages He might show the incompa-
rable riches of His grace, expressed in His kindness to us in Christ
Jesus. For it is by grace you have been saved, through faith—and
this is not from yourselves, it is the gift of God – not by works, so
that no one can boast."*

– Ephesians 2:4-9

More Than Restored

Salvation is only the first step. It is the beginning of your restoration, the foundation of your divine destiny. God does not see you as you see yourself — flawed, broken, and unworthy. He sees beyond that. He sees the reality of you as the person He created you to be: Redeemed, restored, and filled with His Spirit.

Despite what you may have been taught, God does not ask you to clean up your life before coming to Him. He does not demand good works or acts as a prerequisite for salvation. He asks only for your belief and acceptance of what His Son did on your behalf. And when you come to Him, then He begins the work of transforming you into the person He created you to be. And one of the most important things for you to understand is that your transformation is a process:

"He who began a good work in you will carry it on to completion until the day of Christ Jesus."

– Philippians 1:6

God knew your weaknesses, infirmities, and natural proclivities long before you were born. Yet, He chose you and adopted you out of love because you are more than that, and your value to Him is not the measure of your good deeds minus your bad ones. In **Ephesians 1:3-5**, Paul writes:

"Praise be to the God and Father of our Lord Jesus Christ, who has blessed us in the heavenly realms with every spiritual blessing in Christ. For he chose us in him before the creation of the world to be holy and blameless in his sight. In love he predestined us for

adoption to sonship through Jesus Christ, in accordance with his pleasure and will."

– Ephesians 1:3-5

You cannot make yourself holy or blameless. And there is more to you than flesh and blood. You are spirit. And it is the Spirit of God entwined with your spirit, working transformation within you that confirms you belong to Him.

It is through that process – and it is a process – that you become who you are created to be.

"For those who are led by the Spirit of God are the children of God. The Spirit you received does not make you slaves, so that you live in fear again; rather, the Spirit you received brought about your adoption to sonship. And by Him we cry, 'Abba, Father.' The Spirit Himself testifies with our spirit that we are God's children. Now if we are children, then we are heirs – heirs of God and co-heirs with Christ, if indeed we share in His sufferings in order that we may also share in His glory."

– Romans 8:14–17

This speaks to the close, intimate relationship with God you are supposed to have, not the distant, casual, superficial affiliation so many are content to settle for.

Out of His incredible love, grace, and patience, God takes you as you are, fallen and broken, bruised and battered, to clean you, heal you, and raise you to the highest place of honor as His child. He provided for your salvation, adoption, and transformation before you were even born.

Through Christ, you are redeemed, restored, and reconciled back to God. You are made perfect in Him and through Him.

And this is just the beginning of the journey He has prepared for you as we shall see in the next chapter.

Chapter Six

Jesus Isn't Returning to Rescue You

I'm just going to be blunt: Jesus is not coming back to stage a rescue mission.

That sentence is going to shake and even anger some believers, but it's the truth. Too many Christians today have bought into the idea that this world is spiraling beyond hope, destined for destruction, and that all we can do is wait it out until Jesus returns to pluck us from the chaos. They scroll through the latest headlines and nod in agreement – wars, disasters, corruption, violence – and conclude that we're all just passengers on a sinking ship.

But that's not the story God is telling.

Jesus isn't returning to evacuate His people from Earth. When He comes back – and He is coming back – it will be to complete the restoration plan that was sealed at the cross. And the "end of the world" won't look much like the doom-and-gloom scenario many have been taught. The truth is more powerful and far more hopeful.

When Adam and Eve fell, sin entered the world and fractured the relationship between God and humanity. But God had a plan for our redemption and restoration.

As I said before, Jesus didn't die just to save you from hell and His sacrifice wasn't just about getting you into Heaven. It was about bringing Heaven to Earth. He did what He did to empower you to live victoriously and to partner with Him. He restored your access to the Father and re-established your authority to steward and reclaim the Earth for the Kingdom of God.

Restoration Is Taking Root

There's no denying the world is in a chaotic state. But with spiritual eyes, you can look beyond the noise and see that underneath the surface, God is moving. Seeds of divine revelation and restoration are starting to break through. Prophecies are being fulfilled. Prayers that have been lifted for generations are being answered. But there's a catch: Much of what God is doing in this season isn't coming through traditional religious channels or institutional oversight.

God is raising up individuals with hearts and minds to follow the direct guidance of the Holy Spirit; people who aren't bound by religious rituals but are in intimate relationship with and fully surrendered to Him.

Many won't recognize what's happening because it doesn't fit inside the box of what they think "church" should look like. But make no mistake, the Ekklesia — the true Body of Christ — is moving and growing. Your spiritual growth isn't about where you sit on Sunday; it's about whether the Spirit is alive and active in you.

Remember, belonging to a church or a denomination doesn't make you part of the Body of Christ. It is the Spirit of God entwined with your spirit that confirms you are His.

Jesus Is Waiting For You To Move

Let's be honest. For many, Christianity has become a spectator sport. Church attendance has replaced genuine engagement with God. Believers sit in pews, listen to sermons, sing songs, and then return to their lives unchanged, wondering why they still feel spiritually empty.

And because of this, too many churches – congregants and clergy – mirror the brokenness of the world instead of reflecting the power and presence of God. They focus their attention on foreboding and anxiety, rather than fixing their attention on the promises and provisions of God. They're powerless.

Instead of stepping into the authority God has given us, they're sitting back, waiting for Jesus to come and "fix" it all. But here's the truth: **Jesus already accomplished the fixing at the cross.**

"But our High Priest offered himself to God as a single sacrifice for sins, good for all time. Then he sat down in the place of honor at God's right hand. There he waits until his enemies are humbled and made a footstool under his feet. For by that one offering he forever made perfect those who are being made holy."
– Hebrews 10:12-14

Jesus is seated at the right hand of the Father. He's not pacing heaven, wringing His hands. So, "Who is He waiting on to humble his enemies and make them a footstool under His feet? He's waiting – for *us*. He's waiting for His people, those "being made holy," to grow in maturity and partner with Him to put in place all that He came to achieve and finish the work of establishing the Kingdom of Heaven on Earth.

Let that sink in. Jesus isn't waiting to swoop in and save you. He's waiting for **you** to step into the authority He's already given you.

"The highest heavens belong to the Lord, but the earth He has given to mankind."

– Psalm 115:16

From the beginning, God entrusted humanity with the stewardship of the Earth. Although we lost our authority after the fall, that commission didn't disappear. Jesus reclaimed our authority and power to meet our assignment, and now more than ever, it's on us to carry it forward. In His name, and by the power of the Holy Spirit, we recovered the divine authority of the Earth that had been lost in the fall.

Christ restored to us the right to claim and steward the Earth, but like the Israelites standing on the edge of the Promised Land, we must be willing to *take* it. That might sound intimidating, but remember David facing Goliath:

"The battle is the Lord's."

– 1 Samuel 17:47

Our part is to move forward in faith.

"What then shall we say in response to these things? If God is for us, who can be against us?"

— Romans 8:31

Your calling isn't to survive until Jesus returns. It's to **advance** the Kingdom on Earth, to be **salt and light**, to be a reflection of the love and character of God, in a world that desperately needs it.

Remember, *"The Kingdom of God is within you."* (See **Luke 17:21**) And the authority of heaven is in your hands. The Holy Spirit resides within you, and you were born for such a time as this. Are you ready to trust God and move forward to bring God's Kingdom into the spaces you influence?

In Part II: Religion vs Relationship, we'll examine what this looks like in practical terms. Chances are, living a life that's centered and focused around a real relationship with God doesn't look the way you've been taught it should.

Part II:

Religion vs Relationship

LEMOND PUBLISHING

Chapter Seven

A Relationship Restored Through Christ

As we've seen, humanity was created to walk with God, to know Him personally, and to be His progeny. But sin disrupted our divine connection, severing the intimacy we were created to enjoy. This brokenness led to layers of separation: Humanity's relationship with God became governed by laws, rituals, sacrifices, and priests who were intermediaries between the Lord and his people. But what was all but lost in time and between those layers was the fact that their purpose was to point to a Savior who would come and repair the gap.

Under the Old Covenant, these things served as temporary means of atonement, pointing forward to a greater, permanent solution. **Hebrews 10:1** explains it clearly:

"The law is only a shadow of the good things that are coming – not the realities themselves. For this reason, it can never, by the same

sacrifices repeated endlessly year after year, make perfect those who
draw near to worship."

— Hebrew 10:1

The sacrifices of bulls and goats could never cleanse humanity from sin. They were placeholders, symbols of something far greater to come.

That "greater" was Jesus Christ. His sacrifice on the cross was the ultimate fulfillment of the Old Covenant. As **Hebrews 9:12** tells us,

"He did not enter by means of the blood of goats and calves; but
He entered the Most Holy Place once for all by His own blood, thus
obtaining eternal redemption."

— Hebrews 9:12

When Christ declared, **"It is finished."** (**John 19:30**), He wasn't just referring to His earthly life. He was proclaiming the completion of God's redemptive plan – the old system of sacrifice and mediation was no longer necessary. The veil in the temple, which had separated humanity from the Holy of Holies, was torn in two from top to bottom (see **Matthew 27:51**), signifying that the way to God's presence was now open for all.

Jesus fulfilled the Father's plan to restore what had been lost – specifically, man's direct and unmediated relationship with Him. His purpose was more than granting salvation; He restored the intimacy that sin had robbed humanity of. The way back to God was made clear, the barriers that had stood between God and His people were removed, and our divine connection with Him was reestablished.

The New Covenant, which replaced the former, was not based on external laws like the old one, but on internal transformation. Jeremiah had prophesied this moment centuries earlier when he wrote,

"I will put My law in their minds and write it on their hearts. I will be their God, and they will be My people."

— Jeremiah 31:33

Jesus ushered in a new era where God's presence would no longer dwell in temples made by human hands, but within the hearts of believers.

Under this New Covenant, our relationship with God is no longer dependent on rituals OR mediated by earthly priests or others. As **1 Timothy 2:5** affirms:

"For there is one God and one mediator between God and mankind, the man Christ Jesus."

— 1 Timothy 2:5

The need for religious intermediaries has been replaced by the indwelling presence of the Spirit of God, who connects us directly to our Heavenly Father.

The Holy Spirit is the linchpin of the New Covenant for you and I, the very presence of God abiding within us. Jesus emphasized the importance of the Spirit's role when He told His disciples, in **John 16:7**:

"It is better for you that I go away. If I do not go away, the Helper will not come to you; but if I go, I will send Him to you."

— John 16:7

Why would Jesus say that? Because the Holy Spirit would do for every believer what Jesus, in His earthly ministry, did for those He physically encountered, which was to guide, teach, and heal. The Spirit would go even further, however: The Spirit would empower us for a life of intimacy with God.

The Holy Spirit is not just a vague force or an occasional influence; the Spirit is the active presence of God in the believer's life. Jesus described Him as *"the Spirit of truth"* who will *"guide you into all truth"*. (**John 16:13**) The Spirit is your Teacher, illuminating the Word of God and helping you to understand its meaning and application in your life. Without the Holy Spirit, Scripture remains just words on a page; with the Spirit, the Word becomes alive, active, and deeply personal.

The Apostle Paul captures this beautifully in **1 Corinthians 2:12-14:**

"What we have received is not the spirit of the world, but the Spirit who is from God, so that we may understand what God has freely given us. This is what we speak, not in words taught us by human wisdom but in words taught by the Spirit, explaining spiritual realities with Spirit-taught words."

— 1 Corinthians 2:12-14

It is through the Holy Spirit that we discern God's will, experience His presence, and grow in spiritual maturity.

The Holy Spirit's Transformative Power

One of the most significant roles of the Holy Spirit is His work of transformation. While religion typically emphasizes behavior modification — trying harder, doing better, and adhering to a set of rules, the Holy Spirit focuses on and is the catalyst for spiritual transformation. The Spirit renews you from the inside out. **Ephesians 4:23-24** calls us to:

"...be made new in the attitude of your minds; and to put on the new self, created to be like God in true righteousness and holiness."
– Ephesians 4:23-24

This transformation goes well beyond behavior modification and is not something you can achieve on your own. As **2 Corinthians 3:18** explains:

"And we all, who with unveiled faces contemplate the Lord's glory, are being transformed into His with ever-increasing glory, which comes from the Lord, who is the Spirit."
– 2 Corinthians 3:18

The Holy Spirit changes you, not by your determination and striving, but by His power and presence in your life.

Scripture Comes Alive Through the Spirit

It's disheartening to me to see how many believers struggle to connect with Scripture, finding it dry, confusing, or irrelevant. This disconnect stems from approaching the Bible as mere literature rather than living revelation. Understanding Scripture isn't an intellectual pursuit; it's a spiritual encounter. The Bible itself declares:

"For the word of God is alive and active. Sharper than any double-edged sword, it penetrates even to dividing soul and spirit, joints and marrow; it judges the thoughts and attitudes of the heart."

– Hebrews 4:12

Without the guidance of the Holy Spirit, the Bible remains a closed book. The Spirit reveals the truth we need for each moment, making the Word personally relevant and actionable in our lives. This isn't about offering a token prayer for guidance before reading; it's about cultivating a continuous, intimate relationship with God where the Spirit actively speaks and leads.

Unfortunately, many churches downplay the Holy Spirit's role because He defies human control. Yet, Scripture reminds us that the Spirit is God's deposit, guaranteeing our inheritance. (See **Ephesians 1:13-14**.) God isn't distant; He is to be engaged with and praised. And the Holy Spirit is central to that engagement.

Approaching Scripture without the Spirit is inconsistent with its divine origin. The same Spirit who inspired the Word is the One who illuminates it for you. God's Word is multidimensional and alive. It unfolds across time. Prophetic words spoken to ancient Israel weren't static; they had immediate relevance <u>AND</u> future fulfillment because His living words transcend time and span eternity.

The Holy Spirit makes Scripture personal. He highlights verses that speak directly to your situations, convicts you where and when changes are needed, and breathes hope where you feel hopeless. He helps you see beyond the text to grasp God's heart and apply His truth to your life. Jesus affirmed this when He said:

"The words I have spoken to you – they are full of the Spirit and life."

– John 6:63

To truly encounter God through His Word, you must learn to depend on the Holy Spirit – not as an afterthought, but as The Essential Guide to all truth.

Chapter Eight

When Church Isn't Working

T hroughout my life, I've encountered many faces and stories of people struggling and searching for something more in their faith and relationship to God. Sheila, Karen, and Thomas, for instance, each have stories that represent a familiar tale in the tapestry of spiritual seeking that crosses cultural boundaries.

Their experiences reflect wider struggles of finding true solace and meaning in one's spiritual journey, and set against the backdrop of global shifts in religious engagement, they pave the way for a deeper exploration of what it means to have a personal encounter with God.

You may relate to one of them.

Sheila was raised in the warmth of a close-knit church community and had always embraced her faith as a cornerstone of her identity. However, as years passed, the rituals and sermons that once gave her a sense of purpose began to feel mechanical and scripted. She found herself going through the motions, and she felt her prayers began to reflect an emptiness of a faith that no longer spoke to her heart.

It wasn't just the repetitiveness of the rituals; it was the growing realization that her spiritual practice lacked the authenticity and personal connection she craved. Sheila yearned for a faith that resonated not just with her joys, but her life's struggles as well. Somehow, she inherently knew that she needed a faith that was alive and evolving, not static and confined within the walls of the traditions she had grown up in.

Her journey had begun to feel like a dance: Two steps forward, one step back. She was raised with the hymns and prayers of a traditional church, clinging to them like a lifeline. Yet, as she grew into adulthood, Sheila wrestled with a faith that felt more like a childhood aspiration than a living reality. She yearned for more, but the sermons and Bible teachings that were once a source of comfort now felt hollow.

It's not that she wanted to let go of what she grew up believing; she just couldn't continue to hold on to something that didn't feel real anymore.

Then there's Karen, whose experience in her large suburban church painted a different, yet equally troubling, picture. Surrounded by hundreds of fellow believers every Sunday, she nevertheless felt an overwhelming sense of isolation. The smiles were friendly, the greetings warm, but she couldn't shake the fact that her connections with fellow members lacked depth.

Karen's church bustled with activities and programs, but missed the core of what she sought – a community where she could feel safe in being and expressing herself, and the doubts she was having.

Her involvement in various church groups, initially a quest for fellowship, slowly turned into a realization that true community – one where individuals are seen, heard, and valued – was missing. Without this real connection, her church began to feel more like a social club than a family of faith. What she found herself craving was a community where her doubts and fears could surface without judgment, and where she could find support and kinship on a deeper level.

On the surface, Karen was the very picture of a devoted church member, always there, always involved. But inside, she was adrift in a sea of faces, completely surrounded yet soulfully alone. In the bustle of church activities, she searched for a connection that went deeper than polite smiles and small talk after service. She had a hunger for a genuine relationship, not just with people, but with God.

The whole situation kept her awake at night.

Thomas, on the other hand, represented a different kind of struggle. A young professional in a large city, he found the teachings of his church increasingly out of sync with his reality. His denomination's doctrinal tenets seemed disconnected from modern life's complexities. He struggled to apply the biblical principles taught on Sundays to his challenges throughout the week.

Simply put, the messages, steeped in tradition, didn't address the difficulties he faced daily and lacked the practical guidance Thomas needed for navigating his career, relationships, and personal growth. This disconnect led to a sense of disillusionment, and he began to view his church experience as an obligation rather than a source of spiritual nourishment.

Where did his faith fit in a world of rapid change, of moral complexities, and digital landscapes? Thomas's story is a quest for relevance, for a faith that speaks to the here and now.

As I said previously, Sheila, Karen, and Thomas's experiences are not isolated and not mere anecdotes. They represent a growing trend of disillusionment and disconnection with traditional religious practices.

Statistics over the past four decades paint a telling picture of this shift. According to a 2021 Gallup poll, church membership in the United States, which stood at 70% in 1999, saw a decline to 47% by 2020 [1]. This decline is not just a number; it's a significant shift away from traditional church involvement and represents millions of individuals, each with their own story of faith and struggle.

It's a profound narrative of spiritual seeking and shifting perspectives in our country. Millions are leaving the church, but you might be surprised to learn that they are not abandoning their faith.

They consider themselves Christians who simply "don't go to church." By conservative estimates, there are now over 30 million people who identify as such in the United States alone. To put that in perspective, that is nearly one in every 10 people you pass on the street.

Not one in every 10 believers, but almost one in every 10 people.

There are seeking individuals in every church, temple, synagogue, mosque, or whatever they call their house of worship, people in every denomination, in every religion, who have come to realize that the path that they are following or what they are doing is not fulfilling; not meeting the need within them that cries out to God. Something has been missing in their lives, and they have a longing for more than man-made tradition, doctrine, or theology.

Something deep within them is calling out for God.

And God is answering. He is showing up personally, and their lives are being transformed by direct, unmediated interaction with Him.

My personal experiences, along with the stories of Sheila, Karen, and Thomas, underscore a fundamental truth I've long known: It's a personal encounter with God that truly transforms one's faith and life.

While their stories illustrate the spiritual challenges many believers face within institutionalized religion, they also expose a deeper issue inherent in many modern faith practices: Human efforts to reach God through rituals, traditions, and institutions are falling short of cultivating the intimacy with God that we are designed to experience. As well-intentioned as these structures might be, they aren't meeting the need we were designed for or the capacity we have within.

Sheila's longing for authenticity, Karen's yearning for true community, and Thomas's desire for relevance are not isolated struggles. Their experiences resonate with countless believers who find themselves caught in the rhythms of religious routines that fail to speak to the depths of their hearts. Rituals, traditions, and institutions can inadvertently create distance rather than draw individuals closer to the divine. While not inherently wrong, they easily become barriers rather than bridges to intimacy with God.

A Failing Framework

For many, church practices create a framework for their faith but fail to provide the dynamic relationship with God that we need and so many desperately crave. Rituals can become mechanical, leaving believers wondering why their faith no longer stirs their souls. Institutional structures can lack the depth of connection needed to foster genuine spiritual growth, and traditions can become outdated and irrelevant.

The heart of the issue is that these systems often focus on external practices – attending services, participating in programs, adhering to rules – while neglecting the internal transformation that comes by way of direct, personal communion with God through the Holy Spirit.

When faith becomes more about "doing" than "being," it loses its vitality and power.

The danger lies in mistaking the structure for the substance. Attending church, singing hymns, or following denominational traditions can be meaningful, but they are not the ultimate goal. These practices are meant to point us toward God, not replace a direct relationship with Him. When the focus shifts from God Himself to the framework that has been built around Him, the inevitable result is disillusionment, burnout, and spiritual stagnation.

For many, the realization of this disconnect leads to a painful reckoning. It's not that they've lost their faith; rather, they've come to see that the path they've been following isn't changing anything. It's not leading them to true transformation or the deeper relationship with God they desire. They aren't experiencing the real, lasting change in themselves that they've longed for – the kind of transformation that reshapes the heart, renews the mind, and revitalizes the spirit.

Instead, people often feel stuck, as though their spiritual growth has plateaued despite their best efforts to stay engaged in church activities and rituals. This growing awareness is one of the reasons so many believers are leaving institutionalized religion [1] – not because they've abandoned God, but because they're searching for something more.

Many don't even know what that more is. But I can tell you that most are seeking a faith that breathes life into their everyday existence, a relationship that moves them beyond mere religious routine and into the profound, life-changing presence of God Himself.

As bleak as this picture may seem, it is in this very longing, this hunger for something more, that the seeds of transformation are sown. The stories of Sheila, Karen, and Thomas, as well as the growing numbers of believers stepping away from institutionalized religion, reveal an underlying reality: Humanity's deepest need is not for more rituals or traditions, but for a personal, intimate relationship with God.

This longing is not new. It's woven into the fabric of who we are, a reflection of the original design God intended for humanity. From the very beginning, God's desire has been for intimacy with His creation. He didn't create us to follow lifeless rituals or to rely on intermediaries to connect with Him. He created us to walk and talk with Him, to know Him personally, and to experience His love firsthand.

Humanity's attempts to bridge the gap have fallen short. Religious systems, for any value they might have, can never restore the intimacy with God we were created for.

This is why personal encounters with God are so important. They bypass the limitations of human understanding and go straight to the heart. When God shows up personally in a person's life, as He is doing for many today, the impact is undeniable. Lives are changed, not through programs or traditions, but through the power of a direct relationship with the Creator.

This is a truth that millions around the world are discovering. And it's a truth that has the power to reignite faith, heal wounds, and lead believers into a vibrant, dynamic bond with God. The call isn't to abandon all forms of organized worship but to put them in their proper place: As tools that support your faith, not as substitutes for the intimate divine connection you were created to have.

If you're feeling lost, disillusioned, or disconnected, the answer isn't found in doing more of the same. It's found in stepping away from the noise, the routines, and the expectations... and seeking God directly. It's about stripping away the layers of man-made religion and rediscovering the simplicity and beauty of walking with God in a personal, transformative relationship.

This kind of relationship is possible, even in the midst of spiritual struggles. God is waiting to meet each of you where you are, to heal your wounds, to speak to your heart, and to lead you into an abundant life.

The question is, are you willing to let go of whatever's been holding you back and step into the freedom and intimacy of a direct relationship with Him?

The answer to that question could change everything.

---

1. References:[1] Gallup, Inc. "U.S. Church Membership Falls Below Majority for First Time." Gallup.com, 29 Mar. 2021. https://news.gallup.com/poll/341963/church-membership-falls-below-majority-first-time.aspx

Chapter Nine

The Rise of Institutionalized Religion

How Did They Miss It?

A s a teenager, I wrestled with what struck me as a fundamental question: How could the religious leaders in Jesus' time — those entrusted with guiding God's people — be so profoundly out of sync with His message and mission? These were the people who should have been closest to God's heart, and yet they were often His fiercest opponents. How did they miss it?

That question eventually led to another, even graver concern as I grew older: *How do we know that today's spiritual leaders and church institutions aren't making the same mistakes?

As I've mentored and coached believers who struggle to experience spiritual breakthroughs, the disconnect I've seen repeatedly is rooted in institutional religion itself. Despite sincere intentions, churches often perpetuate patterns that hinder spiritual growth rather than nurture it. These patterns trace their origins back to the very foundation of the institutional Church — a foundation that has been flawed from the start.

Woven into the fabric of "the Church" are issues rooted in control, pride, fear, and insecurity. These traits have shaped the organization's hierarchical systems, creating structures that often suffocate the work of the Holy Spirit rather than empower it. While God's grace can and does work through these institutions, the consequences of these flaws have reverberated for generations.

Today, the church is rife with division, stagnation, and spiritual weakness. It is often unable to fulfill the transformative role that Christ intended.

Flawed Beginnings

To grasp how the Ekklesia – God's Spirit-led gathering of believers – was institutionalized into the system we now know as "The Church" and practically neutralized of its power and influence, we must examine its early foundations. This isn't about the vibrant movement of the Holy Spirit that began at Pentecost or the organic spread of believers who called themselves followers of "The Way." That was pure and powerful, a divine outpouring of God's intention. What followed, however, reveals how human nature (and perhaps demonic influence) sought to take what was spiritual and transform it into something institutional.

Specifically, Rome took what was meant to be a Spirit-led community and imposed its own hierarchical and administrative framework, co-opting the Ekklesia for a structured, institutionalized system. This was the birth of what we now call "The Church." While the original movement of "The

Way" reflected the freedom, diversity, and power of the Holy Spirit, the systems that followed began to mold a crusade that was something far more rigid and human-driven.

Over time, cultural influences and the desire for control and order replaced Christ's original design for a Spirit-led body of believers. The result was a shift from a living, spiritual organism – a community empowered by the very Spirit of God – to formal organizations defined by hierarchy and tradition. The Ekklesian movement was absorbed and its essence diluted, as human understanding, ambition, and societal norms began to dictate the structure and function of what Christ had intended to remain dynamic and Spirit-led.

Let's take a peek at a few examples and influences that set the direction of the church:

CLEMENT OF ROME (C. 35–99 AD)

Around the same time that John wrote the Revelation (95 AD), Clement of Rome, one of the earliest leaders of the Roman church, addressed a letter to the church in Corinth, emphasizing the importance of order and obedience to church leaders. He is credited with introducing the concept of hierarchical leadership within the Christian community. While he advocated for unity and stability in the church, his writings also introduced the idea of a clear distinction between clergy and laity.

Clement's teachings argued that leadership within the church was divinely appointed and hierarchical in nature. He compared church leadership to the Old Testament priesthood, reinforcing the idea that certain individuals held a higher spiritual status and authority. This analogy to the priestly system of the Old Covenant marked a departure from the egalitarian, Spirit-led model of the early Ekklesia.

In short, Clement's writings provided the foundation for a hierarchical church structure that placed authority in the hands of a select few, diminishing the role of the Holy Spirit in guiding individuals and the community as a whole.

IGNATIUS OF ANTIOCH (C. 35–108 AD)

Ignatius, a bishop of Antioch, was one of the most vocal proponents of a hierarchical church structure. In his letters to various churches, Ignatius repeatedly emphasized the authority of bishops. He declared that the bishop should be regarded as the ultimate spiritual leader, comparing the bishop to Christ Himself.

Ignatius also advocated for strict obedience to the clergy, arguing that no church activity, should take place without the bishop's approval. His teachings effectively centralized authority within the office of the bishop, sidelining the role of elders and the broader community of believers.

Ignatius's insistence on the supreme authority of bishops marked a significant shift from the Spirit-led, decentralized model of the early Ekklesia to a rigid hierarchy. His teachings marginalized the role of ordinary believers and established a precedent for institutional control.

IRENAEUS OF LYONS (C. 130–202 AD)

Irenaeus, a bishop in what is now France, is best known for his defense of orthodox Christianity against heresies, particularly Gnosticism. While his efforts to preserve sound doctrine were commendable, Irenaeus also introduced the concept of "apostolic succession." This idea asserted that only those ordained by a lineage of bishops tracing back to the apostles had the authority to teach and lead the church.

While apostolic succession was intended to protect the church from false teaching, it also created an exclusive hierarchy that excluded lay believers from meaningful participation in ministry. It reinforced the idea that spiritual authority was centralized in the clergy, further distancing ordinary Christians from the Spirit-led model of the early Ekklesia.

Irenaeus's emphasis on apostolic succession established the institutional church as the sole arbiter of spiritual truth, limiting individual believers' access to direct revelation and the Spirit's guidance.

TERTULLIAN (C. 155–240 AD)

Tertullian, often regarded as the "Father of Latin Christianity," was a prominent theologian and apologist in the early church. (An apologist is a theologian who defends the Catholic faith through apologetics, the intellectual defense of Christianity.) Based in Carthage, Tertullian's writings significantly shaped Christian theology and laid the foundation for much of Western Christianity. He was one of the first to introduce and develop key theological concepts, such as the Trinity and the dual nature of Christ.

However, Tertullian also reinforced the idea of a distinct divide between clergy and laity. While he contributed much to the defense and development of the faith, his views helped establish a formal, hierarchical structure in the church that placed significant power and authority in the hands of clergy. Tertullian argued that the clergy, by virtue of their office, held a unique and superior standing in the church. This fostered a growing dependence on ordained leaders to mediate between God and the people.

In addition, Tertullian was a strong proponent of rigid moral and doctrinal standards. This emphasis on strict rules and ecclesiastical authority sowed the seeds for an institutionalized church that prioritized control and conformity over Spirit-led community and personal relationship with God.

CYPRIAN OF CARTHAGE (C. 200–258 AD)

Cyprian, a prominent bishop of Carthage, played a crucial role in solidifying the hierarchical structure of the church. He rose to prominence and became known for his writings and leadership during a time of significant persecution and division in the church.

Cyprian strongly believed in the authority of bishops and the centrality of the institutional church. He famously declared, "He cannot have God as his Father who does not have the Church as his Mother," asserting that salvation was inextricably tied to the authority of the church. This statement elevated the institutional church to a position of supreme spiritual authority, making it the gatekeeper of salvation.

His views entrenched the idea that the institutional church, rather than the Holy Spirit, was the ultimate authority in the believer's life. His teachings laid the groundwork for the centralized, hierarchical structure that would dominate Christianity for centuries and limit the Spirit's direct work in individual believers.

AUGUSTINE OF HIPPO (C. 354–430 AD)

Augustine, one of the most influential theologians in Christian history, made significant contributions to Christian thought, particularly in the areas of original sin, grace, and the nature of the church. However, Augustine also played a key role in merging church and state, advocating for the use of political power to enforce religious orthodoxy.

Augustine's writings supported the idea that the church had the authority to use coercion to bring wayward believers into compliance. This set a precedent for the persecution of dissenters and the centralization of power within the institutional church.

While Augustine's theology shaped much of Western Christianity, his emphasis on institutional authority and the blending of church and state reinforced the hierarchical systems that the church had established.

I could go on but I'm sure you get the point.

These early developments shaped the Roman Catholic Church, establishing a hierarchical structure that emphasized control, conformity, and ritual over the freedom in Christ that the early "Ekklesia" enjoyed. Now, it may be tempting to lay the problem within the Roman Catholic Church and leave it there, but we still have to take the Reformation and Protestantism into account.

The Protestant Reformation

The Protestant Reformation, which began in the 16th century, was a monumental movement in the history of Christianity, breaking away from the authoritarianism of the Catholic Church. Reformers such as Martin Luther, John Calvin, Huldrych Zwingli, and others had a vision of liberating the Christian faith from the institutional grip of Rome, which had long established a hierarchy that dictated how believers should experience and express their relationship with God.

The Reformers successfully initiated a sweeping change that reshaped Christianity, but unfortunately, they retained many of the hierarchical structures and institutional characteristics of the "Mother Church." The underlying reliance on human authority persisted. Protestantism largely replicated similar levels of control and hierarchy within its ranks. Bishops, councils, and committees became a new kind of clergy class, replacing the old but retaining the structure.

Although their theology differed, their approach to authority mirrored the very system they had intended to reform. This unintended carryover hindered the potential of the Reformation to restore the original, participatory model of the early Ekklesia.

The result of this retained hierarchy has been a constraint on the movements of God. Just as the Catholic hierarchy once limited how and where people could experience God, the newer Protestant structures imposed their own limitations. Denominational doctrines and administrative approval restricted movements of the Spirit of God as governing bodies became the arbiters of spiritual experience, defining and dictating what was acceptable.

Even as great men of God, the Wesleys, George Whitefield, Jonathan Edwards, Gilbert Tennent, Cotton Mather, and others in the 18th century, initiated movements that turned large numbers of people to Christ, they were building organizations on a less than "perfect" foundation initiated not by God but by man.

Though perhaps more decentralized than Catholicism, Protestantism largely imposed restrictions on individual believers' ability to fulfill the personal moves of the Spirit in their lives. Like ancient Israel's dependency on a priestly class, and like the Catholic church they broke away from, Protestant believers were taught to look to their leaders for direction at the expense of seeking the Holy Spirit's guidance themselves.

These circumstances all point to a common theme: Humanity's tendency to rely on religion, rituals, and self-effort instead of trusting in God's provision for transformation and pursuing a genuine relationship with Him.

But God is not looking for external displays of devotion; He desires your heart.

Chapter Ten

Beyond Religion

Humanity has long wrestled with how to relate to God. This struggle isn't new — it traces back to Adam and Eve and echoes throughout history, from the Old Testament to the establishment of the Church, through the Protestant Reformation, and right into our modern lives. Repeatedly, mankind has tried to define the terms of interaction with the Almighty, building rules, rituals, and theological frameworks to reach out to God on human terms.

But here's the hard truth: All these efforts, however well-intentioned, miss the point. The essence of religion is man's attempt to reach God by our own means, to manage and control our relationship with Him.

And that's not what He intended.

Many believers have a relationship with God that is clouded by the layers of religion they've inherited. Instead of a direct, vibrant connection with the Lord, they're left navigating traditions, rules, and rituals that, for many, feel more like barriers than bridges. The problem is that religion, at its core, is man's way of defining the terms and conditions of how we interact with God rather than simply receiving the relationship He freely offers.

This focus on religion, especially "Institutional Christianity," often leads to what I call "religiosity" – a devotion to the structure rather than to God Himself. Doctrines and traditions take center stage, pushing aside the personal, transforming power of the Holy Spirit. Many churches still operate under the old covenant model, focusing on external actions and behaviors rather than embracing the New Covenant, which invites conversion through a direct divine relationship.

This can be difficult to comprehend because it often challenges a good deal of conventional church practices. But God isn't interested in us just following rules or trying to be "good" on our own. He desires to bring true transformation through the Holy Spirit. Religion tries to modify our behavior from the outside, but God works from the inside out, changing our hearts and minds so that our actions naturally align with His will. It's a shift from doing things to please God to simply being in relationship with Him and allowing His Spirit to transform us.

Unfortunately, over time, many religious institutions and leaders have unintentionally – and sometimes intentionally – put themselves in the place of the Holy Spirit. They've become the gatekeepers, controllers, and wardens, overshadowing the intimate, personal relationship God desires with each of us. The Holy Spirit's role (to guide, teach, and empower) gets replaced by rules, regulations, human expectations, and intermediaries, and we're left with something less than God intended, that is hollow and powerless.

But it doesn't have to be this way.

When God sent His Son, He didn't offer us a new religious system to join. Christ offered Himself. He came to restore what Adam and Eve lost: A direct, personal, unbroken relationship with God. Jesus came to mend the broken connection between us and our Creator.

If God had wanted to establish a new religion, He could have easily done so through the Pharisees. They already had their elaborate and complex laws, rituals, and traditions. But Christ didn't affirm their system – He challenged it. He confronted their legalism and self-righteousness, exposing how they had missed the heart of God. In **Matthew 23:23**, He told them...

"You have neglected the more important matters of the law — justice, mercy, and faithfulness."
— Matthew 23:23

Their meticulous adherence to the law could not cover the absence of love, mercy, and humility in their hearts. God was after more. A lot more.

When Christ died on the cross and the temple curtain was torn in two, it signified the end of the old covenant system and the beginning of the new; the restoration of direct access to God since Eden, thanks to the work of Christ and the indwelling of the Holy Spirit.

This is the heart of the New Covenant. Jesus said in **John 14:6**,

"I am the way, and the truth, and the life. No one comes to the Father except through me."
— John 14:6

He didn't say, "Follow these rules, and you'll find the way," or "Adhere to this doctrine, and you'll know the truth." He pointed to Himself as the way to the Father. The Father's heart has always been for intimacy with His children, and Christ's sacrifice made that possible again.

When you embrace the connection with God that Jesus made possible, you stop striving to check religious boxes or live up to arbitrary standards. Instead, you're transformed by His Spirit from the inside out. This is what **Jeremiah 31:33** and **Hebrews 10:16** are referring to:

"This is the covenant I will make with them after that time, says the Lord. I will put my laws in their hearts, and I will write them on their minds."

— Hebrews 10:16

Getting right with God Is not about self-improvement, personal development, or behavior modification. Everything that we aspire to, or the Godly-character traits that we seek to reflect, as Paul writes in **Galatians 5:22-23**:

"the fruit of the Spirit: love, joy, peace, patience, kindness, goodness, faithfulness, gentleness, and self-control..."

— Galatians 5:22-23

...aren't produced by your will or determination (at least not consistently), but by the Holy Spirit's work in your life.

Religion will always fall short because it focuses on what we do. But a true relationship with God focuses on what He has already done, what He continues to do within us, and how we reflect Him because of those two things.

If you're longing for a more genuine connection with God, it might be time to step back from religious structures and lean into the deeper, more personal relationship He desires to have with you. The Holy Spirit is ready to equip, empower, and transform you in ways you could never achieve on your own. It's a journey of letting go of the "rules" and embracing the divine intimacy that redresses you completely.

God isn't interested in rituals or religious systems. He wants a relationship. He wants your heart. He's already reached down to you through Christ, and now He's inviting you to walk with Him in freedom, intimacy, and love. It's not about trying harder. It's about surrendering to the Holy Spirit and allowing Him to do the transformative work in you.

That is the essence of what it means to move out of rituals and into relationship.

Chapter Eleven

Struggling With The Old Covenants

I 've shared a lot about circumstances since the implementation of the New Covenant. But let's step even further back in history for a bit.

Throughout the Old Testament, we see recurring examples of how the people of God struggled to trust and obey Him. Time and again, Israel tried to take matters into their own hands, often substituting their own ideas for God's clear instructions. These missteps reveal a deep-seated tendency in us to approach God on our terms rather than His, and they demonstrate the futility of religion when it replaces direct relationship with Him.

Here are three key examples.

THE GOLDEN CALF (EXODUS 32)

The story of the golden calf is one of the most infamous examples of Israel's impatience and failure to trust God. After God delivered the Israelites from slavery in Egypt with miraculous signs and wonders, including parting the Red Sea, the people stood at Mount Sinai, where God gave Moses the Ten Commandments. This was a moment of unparalleled closeness between God and His people – He was revealing His covenant to them and providing the framework for their new identity as a holy nation.

But when Moses went up the mountain to meet with God and didn't return for 40 days, the people grew impatient. They began to doubt whether Moses would return at all and whether God was still with them. Despite everything they had witnessed and all that the Lord had done on their behalf – the plagues in Egypt, the parting of the Red Sea, and God's provision of manna and water in the wilderness – their faith failed them. Fear and insecurity crept in, and they decided to take matters into their own hands.

Aaron, the brother of Moses, gave in to their demands to create gods to "go before" them that they could see and perceive; something more to their understanding. Aaron instructed them to collect their gold jewelry, which he melted down to create a golden calf. He even went so far as to proclaim,

> *"These are your gods, Israel, who brought you up out of Egypt."*
> *– Exodus 32:4*

This act of rebellion was a clear violation of the very first two commandments: To have no other gods before the Lord and to avoid making idols.

Why did Israel become impatient? At its core, the problem was a lack of trust in God's timing and a desire to control their situation. They couldn't see what God was doing on the mountain, so they reverted to what felt familiar – an idol, something tangible that they could see and touch. They replaced faith with religion, if you will, creating their own system of worship to fill the void.

The lesson is a pertinent one: When we grow impatient with God or try to force solutions in our own strength and understanding, we risk turning to substitutes that can never satisfy or save us.

KING SAUL'S DISOBEDIENCE (1 SAMUEL 15)

Saul's story is a tragic example of someone who was chosen by God but failed to keep himself aligned with God's purpose. Saul was Israel's first king, chosen not because of his merit but because of God's grace and Israel's insistence on having a human king. The people demanded a king to lead them "like all the other nations," despite God warning them that this desire would lead to hardship. (See)

Nevertheless, God allowed it and chose Saul, a man from the tribe of Benjamin, who stood out for his impressive physical stature and humble beginnings. Saul started as an ideal choice, beginning his governance over Israel with humility and a desire to serve.

However, as his reign progressed, his pride, insecurities, fear of man, and lack of obedience to God grew. One of the clearest examples of this is in 1 Samuel 15, when God commanded Saul to completely destroy the Amalekites, including all their livestock, as an act of divine justice for their long-standing wickedness. But Saul disobeyed. He spared King Agag and kept the best of the livestock, claiming that he intended to use the animals for sacrifices to God.

When confronted by the prophet Samuel, Saul tried to justify his actions, saying,

"The soldiers took sheep and cattle from the plunder, the best of what was devoted to God, to sacrifice them to the Lord your God at Gilgal."

– 1 Samuel 15:21

But Samuel's response exposed Saul's failure to understand what God truly desired:

"Does the Lord delight in burnt offerings and sacrifices as much as in obeying the Lord? To obey is better than sacrifice, and to heed is better than the fat of rams."

– 1 Samuel 15:22

Saul's disobedience revealed a deeper issue: He was more concerned with appearances and human approval than fully trusting and obeying God. By sparing the livestock and the king of the Amalekites, Saul demonstrated that his concerns were more important to him than what God had instructed. This act of rebellion cost him his kingship, and the Spirit of the Lord, which had rested on him, departed from his presence.

Saul's story serves as a cautionary tale of how even those chosen by God can lose their way when they pursue their own agenda or prioritize their understanding over God's instructions. It also underscores the importance of obedience and trust in our relationship with God.

The Prophets' Warnings

Throughout Israel's history, God sent prophets to call His people back to Him when they strayed. These prophets were His messengers, delivering words of correction, warning, and hope. But all too often, the people ignored their messages, choosing instead to follow their own ways or cling to vain religious rituals devoid of a relationship with God.

ISAIAH'S REBUKE OF EMPTY WORSHIP (ISAIAH 1:11-17):

The prophet Isaiah confronted the people of Judah about their meaningless sacrifices and hypocritical worship. While they were meticulously following the sacrificial system, their hearts were far from God. The Lord declared,

"Stop bringing meaningless offerings! Your incense is detestable to me... Learn to do right; seek justice. Defend the oppressed. Take up the cause of the fatherless; plead the case of the widow."
– Isaiah 1:13, 17

This passage reveals God's heart: He is not impressed by outward displays of religion or even superficial obedience to the law. What God desires is a transformed heart that reflects His character through acts of justice, mercy, and compassion.

MICAH'S CALL TO TRUE WORSHIP (MICAH 6:6-8):

The prophet Micah echoed a similar sentiment when he asked,

"With what shall I come before the Lord and bow down before the exalted God? Shall I come before him with burnt offerings, with calves a year old?"
– Micah 6:6

The answer comes in verse 8:

"He has shown you, O mortal, what is good. And what does the Lord require of you? To act justly and to love mercy and to walk humbly with your God."

– Micah 6:8

These powerful statements encapsulate the difference between adhering to religion and engaging in a relationship with God. The Lord isn't looking for ritualistic offerings; He seeks a people who reflect who He is... because they've come to know Him. When you truly begin to know who God is, His personal presence in your life begins a process of inevitable change within you. You cannot help but begin to reflect Him, walking with Him in increasing love, mercy, and humility that flows from Him through you.

That is something too many believers have never realized.

Under the old covenants, the people of Israel relied on priests and kings to mediate their relationship with God and take responsibility for the nation's spiritual direction. The law, sacrifices, and rituals were external mechanisms designed to maintain a connection to Him, but Israel frequently fell back into patterns of idolatry and religious formalism. They repeatedly failed to live up to their part of the covenant's demands.

This led to times of significant spiritual decline, when God's people drifted away from the commandments and fell into idolatry. Other prophets like Elijah, Hezekiah, and Josiah led movements to bring the people back to the worship of Yahweh, but these revivals generally failed to last beyond a generation when, almost habitually, the people fell back into cycles of disobedience and idolatry, and the nation once again had to be called to repentance.

These situations were, in part, a result of the limitations of the old covenants and, in no small part, the very human nature of sinful man and our inherent human inability to uphold it despite their promise and even perhaps their intention to do so.

Israel, as a nation and of their own accord, had repeatedly taken an oath to God that they would do all that the Lord told them to do. See **Exodus 19:8; 24:3,7; Deuteronomy 5:27**; and **Jeremiah 42:6,20** for a few examples.

Israel's spiritual revivals were based on external conformity rather than lasting internal transformation. And so, while a generation may have returned to God under the influence of a godly leader, the revival usually faded when that leader was gone, unable to be sustained by the population themselves.

Then, unlike now, the Holy Spirit did not indwell within individuals. Rather, the Spirit would temporarily rest upon and empower certain leaders or prophets for specific tasks. People did not have the personal, internal guidance of the Spirit of God in the way that believers can now experience under the New Covenant.

And without the permanent indwelling of the Holy Spirit to transform their hearts and minds, the people lacked the internal transformation needed to sustain their faith. As a result, Israel fell into cycles of rebellion, repentance, and revival, unable to uphold or break free from the limitations of the Old Covenant.

This is why the writer of the New Testament book of **Hebrews** explains in chapter 8, verse 6:

"But in fact the ministry Jesus has received is as superior to theirs as the covenant of which he is mediator is superior to the old one, since the new covenant is established on better promises."

– Hebrews 8:6

The "better promises" are the guarantees of a new, intimate, and transformative relationship with God through Jesus Christ. They assure us of direct access to God, internal transformation by the Holy Spirit, complete forgiveness of sins, unconditional grace, and an eternal inheritance.

The Old Covenant highlighted humanity's need for God as well as our inability to meet His standards through works. The New Covenant reveals the heart of God and His desire to meet us where we are, transform us from within, and restore the relationship He always intended.

The relationship you can have with God now is starkly different. The Old Covenant was focused on external laws written on tablets of stone. It required strict adherence to the Law, but it couldn't change the heart. Blessings were contingent upon obedience to the Law (see **Deuteronomy 28**), and failure to comply brought curses.

Under the New Covenant, God's laws are written on your heart and mind, and the Holy Spirit transforms you from the inside out, leading to genuine change, not mere outward compliance. The fulfillment and upholding of the covenant is based on His grace, not your effort. Your salvation and right standing with God come through your faith in Jesus, not through your works. (See **Ephesians 2:8-9**)

What you do and how you act will change, not because you're simply trying to be and do better, but because you are being positively affected through the ever-increasing intimacy you cultivate with God that is made possible through the Spirit of God, as we'll examine further in the next chapter.

Chapter Twelve

The Criticality of The Holy Spirit

The death and resurrection of Christ achieved God's purpose, marking the fulfillment of the old covenants and the establishment of a new one. At the moment Jesus gave His life on the cross, something extraordinary occurred. Until that point, only the high priest could enter the innermost room of the temple – the Holy of Holies – and only once a year to make atonement for the sins of the people. This sacred space, both near to and separated from God, was shielded by a thick, woven curtain over sixty feet high.

When Christ breathed His last breath, that curtain was torn in two from top to bottom. This was no mere physical act; it was a powerful, symbolic declaration. The old covenant, with its reliance on works, rituals, and human intermediaries, was no longer the way to access God's presence or embodiment. In that moment, the barrier was removed and a way was opened for every believer to engage in direct communion with Him. The tearing of the curtain signified the beginning of the New Covenant, ushered in through Christ's sacrifice.

Through this new covenant, the Holy Spirit now dwells within believers, granting us direct access to the Almighty Himself. By His grace and through the work of the Holy Spirit, rituals and intermediaries were replaced by the intimate, personal relationship with God that is now available to all who believe.

The Spirit's indwelling presence is transformative, renewing hearts, reshaping minds, and leading to spiritual growth that is both profound and lasting. Unlike the old covenant, which relied on external works, the New Covenant is grounded in the work of Jesus, resulting in a deeply personal relationship with God that changed everything for you and I.

The Spirit at Work Through History

The transformative power of the Holy Spirit has been especially evident in the great revivals of the past 300 years. Unlike the generational cycles of revival and falling away experienced by Israel under the old covenant, these more modern movements have had lasting effects because they were rooted in the Spirit's internal work rather than mankind's external conformity.

The First Great Awakening in the 1730s, led by figures like Jonathan Edwards and George Whitefield, awakened the faith of thousands, reshaping culture and society in profound ways. **The Second Great Awakening** in the early 19th century brought renewed fervor for evangelism and social reform. Movements like the Pentecostal and Charismatic revivals of the 20th century, including the Azusa Street Revival, emphasized the gifts of the Holy Spirit, empowering individuals to experience God personally.

These movements demonstrated the Holy Spirit's power to transform lives and communities, yet even they were sometimes constrained by the imposition of religious hierarchies and denominational structures. When human systems attempt to formalize or control the Spirit's work, they often limit its potential, diverting energy into maintaining institutional frameworks at the expense of more fully advancing God's Kingdom.

The Problem With Human Hierarchies

The early Pentecostal movement began as a radical departure from the rigidity of organized religion, embracing the transformative work of the Holy Spirit in each believer's life. It was a movement defined by freedom and authenticity. However, as the movement grew, hierarchies formed, and denominational boundaries were drawn, limiting the Spirit's unrestrained work. Human effort frequently replaced divine leading, diminishing the movement's impact.

Instead of fully embracing the New Covenant, institutional Christianity often cleaves to an old covenant mindset. While well-intentioned, this propensity, born of human effort and intent, can constrain a believer to allow the Spirit to move freely within. Emphasizing rules, rituals, and denominational doctrines over relationship with God reduces divine supernatural moves to something controllable by human standards instead of encouraging the Spirit's transforming work in our lives.

This shifts our focus from the renewal of our hearts and minds through grace to outward behavior and conformity. Faith becomes about meeting institutional standards rather than experiencing the power and reality of a Spirit-led life. As a result, many believers find themselves disconnected from the vibrant relationship with God that Christ restored to them.

Returning to the Spirit-Led Model

The early followers of "The Way" embraced a Spirit-led model of community. They gathered in homes, worshiped together, and shared a fellowship where every believer's God-given gifts were valued. Leadership was fluid, based on spiritual gifting rather than titles or positions of authority. This decentralized approach allowed the Ekklesia to grow explosively, spreading the message of Christ with authenticity and power.

The Kingdom of God was never meant to be confined within institutional walls. The Gospel thrived, and the early Ekklesia flourished because they prioritized direct relationships with God over centralized authority.

By relying directly on the Holy Spirit to lead, we become what we are meant to be: Living, breathing expressions of God's love, grace, and power; conduits of the Kingdom of Heaven that transform lives and impact the world far beyond what human effort could ever achieve.

A New Wineskin

The New Covenant ended reliance on works-based righteousness. Under the old covenant, people struggled to "be good" on their own, and they offered sacrifices for their sins. The New Covenant, however, is about accepting Christ's sacrifice on your behalf and allowing the Holy Spirit to transform and renew you from the inside out. True spiritual growth comes not from striving to meet external standards but from surrendering to the Spirit's work within you.

The Holy Spirit is your ultimate Teacher and Guide, equipping you with divine wisdom, peace, and renewal. Unlike man-created paradigms and systems, the Spirit provides a transformative connection to God that religion cannot replicate. While church can provide fellowship, encouragement, and shared worship, it is not a sure foundation for faith. Your relationship with God must rest on intimacy with Him, through the Spirit, not on theologies, doctrines, or rules.

As such, much of the current infrastructure of Christian religion resembles an "old wineskin" that cannot hold the new wine of revelation or fresh moves of the Spirit without bursting. (See **Luke 5:37**) Churches that are focused on their institutional rules and denominational traditions in preference to following the direct guidance of the Spirit – and encourage their congregants to do the same – are leaving believers spiritually stagnated, disillusioned, and wounded by their experiences.

Christ invites you into something more – a vibrant, dynamic relationship with God, empowered by His Spirit. You can let go of old rituals and traditions that have left you feeling disconnected and embrace intimacy with God. Walk with Him, converse with Him, and approach His throne in confidence whenever you feel you need to. This is part of the abundant life Christ has prepared and restored to you.

Your spiritual life is not about adhering to someone else's conditions for a relationship with God; it's about the terms God set for a relationship with you: Terms of grace, mercy, and love. Under the New Covenant, the Holy Spirit empowers you to walk in alignment with the Kingdom of Heaven and the will of God.

If you've ever felt stuck or hemmed in in church, it's likely because you've been relying on religion to do what only a direct relationship with God can. The good news is that the door to intimacy with Him is always open. The Holy Spirit is ready and waiting for you to turn your attention to the Lord.

While churches and denominations have good intentions, the institutional model too often stifles the very essence of what it means to know and walk with God. When religion gets prioritized over relationship, it creates a religious mindset that obscures and obstructs the Spirit's transformative power.

The key to thriving in your faith is intimacy with God. This relationship is what transforms you – not rituals, not traditions, and not human determination. Put the Holy Spirit in His rightful place as your teacher, guide, and source of truth. Then you can step into the abundant life Jesus promised.

The call of the Ekklesia is to follow the leading of the Spirit. This is the power of the New Covenant and the path to living the life you were created for. When you step into a direct relationship with God, everything begins to change.

Spiritual transformation happens through intimacy with God. It is a product of the Holy Spirit working within you, not through self-effort or external performance.

It is the Spirit who equips, empowers, and renews you, nothing less. When you learn to listen, lean on, and follow God directly, you experience a kind of spiritual growth and transformation that religion cannot provide.

No amount of striving to meet external standards will renew your heart or mind; only the Holy Spirit can do that.

Now, to be perfectly clear, when I refer to the problems of the Church or its issues, I am not saying that churches are bad. I am not anti-church. There is tremendous value in the church experience, including fellowship, sharing, and moving together with a collective sense of purpose. Lifting our voices together to give thanks, express gratitude, and give God glory from our hearts isn't merely an exercise; it brings us into agreement and aligns us with the Heavenly hosts to give Him glory.

Community is crucial and unlocks Heavenly dimensions of power in the spirit that can't be conceived of in the natural. It strengthens and bolsters our souls.

This is the reason we are admonished not to neglect or give up meeting together. (See **Hebrews 10:25**) I fully support church in its proper context, but it is not (and cannot be) the cornerstone of your relationship with God. It is a girder, a pillar for your house that sits upon the bedrock of relationship and intimacy you have with God through the Holy Spirit.

I am simply advising you to be mindful and aware. Be Spirit-led when it comes to selecting a congregation to join or a community to become part of. More on this in Chapter 17.

Now that we've examined how institutional religion has strayed from God's original design, it's time to look inward. Recognizing the limitations of man-made systems is just the beginning. As I've taken pains to point out, transformation happens when, under the guidance of the Holy Spirit, you address areas in your life where a religious mindset has taken root and has supplanted the relationship God desires to have with you.

In the next section, I'll introduce you to a practical, proven framework that will set you on the road and empower you to cultivate intimacy with God. You'll learn how to converse with Him, ask questions, receive answers, and respond to His guidance. This is not about adopting another set of religious practices. It's about learning to converse, allowing His Spirit to speak into every area of your life.

Chapter Thirteen

Now What? Rebuilding Faith, Trust, and Purpose Outside the Walls

I f you've made it this far, chances are there's something in you that just can't keep doing "church" as usual. Maybe you've already stepped away from the church building – quietly, painfully, maybe even with a sigh of relief you can't fully explain. Perhaps you're still hanging on, showing up, singing the songs, nodding at the sermons... but there's a gnawing ache under the surface that says, *"This isn't working anymore."* Maybe you've tasted enough freedom to see how stale the old routine has become, but you're not sure what to do with that realization.

You might feel some relief... but you also feel the tremor of fear that comes with stepping into the unknown.

Because once the sermons fade and the doors shut behind you, what do you do with this new awareness of the Holy Spirit? How do you even begin to live out a faith that isn't dictated by someone else's program, schedule, or tradition? Where do you go when you're done being spoon-fed, but you're still learning how to chew on real spiritual food for yourself?

This isn't just a shift in doctrine or theology. This is personal. You're feeling raw and exposed, standing in a wilderness season with no guidebook, no pastor or priest telling you what to believe. And no guarantees you won't screw it up.

I know exactly what that feels like, because I've been there more than once.

For years, God sent me into churches across denominations, across cities, across the spectrum of what calls itself "Christian community." Some were full of genuine, humble, Spirit-filled people who were a blessing. Places where I continued to grow and help. And others... well, God sent me to those to learn what not to do.

Some places broke my heart, or burned me out, or made me question much of what I thought I knew. Sometimes I stayed too long, because I didn't want to be the one who walked away first. Sometimes I slipped out quietly, shaking the dust off my feet. And sometimes I left in grief, convinced I had somehow failed God by not being able to connect or make a difference.

I didn't always see the situations for what they were: God wasn't sending me into those places to settle down. He was showing me the difference between the noise of religion and the quiet, steady voice of His Spirit.

I've walked with many over the years, people who poured themselves out in service until there was nothing left – people who stayed long past the point of exhaustion, hoping that maybe this time their effort would be enough. But the damage doesn't always come wrapped in obvious spiritual abuse or harsh sermons. Sometimes it's quieter, more insidious. It's the gossip whispered just loud enough for them to hear when they didn't fit the unspoken mold. It's the subtle snubbing of someone who came from the "wrong" side of town, whose clothes, accent, or history didn't match the tidy image the church wanted to project.

I've watched people try to belong in places where the clique walls were high and the doors were only half-open, where acceptance was conditioned on looking, talking, and worshiping exactly like everyone else. I've sat across from hearts that were wounded not because they broke the rules, but because they dared to question them; gently challenging the elders or poking holes in the accepted dogma. All too often, that served as an unwelcome reminder that maybe the status quo wasn't as holy as it pretended to be.

I've tried to help when I've read the confusion on people's faces, the inevitable grief that comes when your mere presence rocks the boat, when you become a threat just for not fitting neatly into others' version of who belongs and who doesn't. And in the end, underneath all of the pain, there's always the same desperate question trembling on their lips:

"Where is God in all this?"

Because here's an uncomfortable truth: Some churches teach you to try harder, perform better, keep smiling while you bleed. They call it discipleship, but it's really just another version of self-help, and when you fail (because you will), the blame is squarely laid on you. The end result is people who are exhausted, guilt-ridden, and convinced that God is an angry parent, standing with His arms crossed, waiting for them to finally get it right.

No wonder so many people walk away.

But there's a catch: Even when you leave, that "spiritual mis-wiring" can stay with you. You might know in your mind that it was the right move, but carry the fear, the guilt, the second-guessing. Your heart still wonders:

- *"Was I wrong to go?"*

- *"Can I even trust God anymore?"*

- *"How do I know I'm not just fooling myself, out here alone?"*

That confusion is real. I've seen it time and again. It's almost like a phantom limb – the system may be gone, but you still feel the old pains, the old doubts.

So I'll tell you straight: You are not alone. You are not crazy. You are not failing God by questioning the walls you once trusted.

This road you're on? It's real. It's hard. But it is not hopeless.And even if you can't feel it yet, there is a path forward. You're not the first to walk it – and you won't be the last.

Healing From What Hurt You

"It wasn't supposed to be like this."

That thought has haunted more of us than you'd think. We just don't always say it out loud. You didn't expect to be wounded by the very people who were supposed to protect and help you grow. You didn't expect that trying to please God would leave you more afraid of Him than close to Him. And you definitely didn't expect to be where you find yourself now: Walking a road alone, unsure who to trust.

But here you are. Wounded. Wary. Wondering if you can even trust God.

I understand. If we're going to talk about rebuilding a Spirit-led relationship with God – and not just slapping a quick "Jesus loves me" bandage over old scars, then we have to talk about the damage first. Because for a lot of people, church hurt isn't just an occasional awkward conversation or an unkind word in the lobby. It's betrayal. It's leaders using Scripture as a weapon. It's being told that real obedience means staying silent when something's wrong. It's the exhaustion of always feeling like you're not quite enough, no matter how much you do.

Sometimes the wounds aren't obvious. Maybe you never had a dramatic exit or a public scandal. But maybe, deep down, you carry a low-grade fear that God is disappointed with you. Or you pause before you pray because you don't "feel holy enough" that day. Or you wonder if the intimacy with God that you hear about from others is only for the spiritually elite... or at least the ones who played by the church's rules and kept their heads down.

These are not small things. They're not quirks or minor flaws in your thinking. They are deep, spiritual wounds. They are distortions of who God actually is. And they take time – and honesty – to heal.

God is *not* like the system that hurt you. He is *not* waiting for you to clean up your mess or "prove" yourself worthy of His love. He is *not* testing you to see if you fail again. He is *not* holding the past against you. He doesn't do that, especially the parts where you tried your best and still got torn up.

Scripture makes it clear:

"The Lord is close to the brokenhearted and saves those who are crushed in spirit."

– Psalm 34:18

"A bruised reed He will not break, and a smoldering wick He will not snuff out."

– Isaiah 42:3 (also quoted in Matthew 12:20)

These verses aren't poetry for a greeting card. They are God describing Himself. They reveal the character of the One who longs to sit with you... not in judgment, but in restoration.

Healing doesn't begin when you explain away the harm "for the sake of unity." It doesn't begin when you feign forgiveness, or slap on a smile, or push past the pain because you think that's what God wants. It begins when you admit the truth: *I was hurt. And it wasn't okay.*

You're allowed to grieve what was done to you. You're allowed to name the harm. You don't need to fix it first. You don't need to run from it, bury it, or rush past it. And yes, you're allowed to feel angry. Even at God. The relationship He wants with you is big enough to hold your full humanity, not just your cleaned-up Sunday theology.

> *"Come to Me, all who are weary and burdened, and I will give you rest. Take My yoke upon you and learn from Me, for I am gentle and humble in heart, and you will find rest for your souls."*
> *– Matthew 11:28–29*

I spent many nights trying to explain away wrongful things that happened – telling myself to just get over it, to forgive, to move on for the sake of the church, the family, the "unity." But breakthrough came when I stopped pretending, stopped asking to make sense of it, and just invited God into the mess. I didn't ask Him to tie it up neatly or give me answers. I just asked Him to sit with me in the ache.

That's what intimacy looks like. It doesn't start with answers... it starts with honesty.

If you're feeling stuck, maybe that's your next step: Not forgiving yet, not fixing, not running. Just telling the truth. *I was hurt. And it wasn't okay.*

You can't rebuild trust on a foundation of denial. But you *can* rebuild it on a foundation of truth. And the truth is: God is still here. Not hovering above you with a disappointed scowl, but kneeling beside you with healing in His hands. He's not asking you to "move on." He's asking you to *move closer.*

God Never Left You Alone

Even when the institution failed you... God didn't.

I know that might be hard to swallow. When you walk away from church, especially after being wounded by the very place you thought you were supposed to find healing, it's easy to feel like you left God, too. There's a good chance that someone even told you that's exactly what you did, as though your faith couldn't survive outside four walls and a Sunday routine. Maybe you've wondered yourself: *Did I fall away? Did I backslide? Did I screw this up so badly that God went quiet?*

Let's kill that lie right here and now.

God never left you. Not when you doubted. Not when you got angry. Not when you stopped talking to Him entirely. Not even when you whispered in the dark that you weren't sure if He was real anymore.

He didn't flinch. He didn't roll His eyes or turn His back. He wasn't intimidated by your grief or your anger. Your questions weren't a threat to His sovereignty. In fact, they might have been the first real thing you said to Him in years.

Here's what religion never taught you: God is not bound to your performance, or your church attendance record, or your ability to quote the "right" verses in the "right" way. He is a relational Being. Always has been. The Holy Spirit doesn't just hang out in pulpits and pews and polished programs – He walks with you on back roads, sits with you in the quiet, waits with you when you have no idea what to pray. He whispers in ways you might not have noticed... yet.

"Even if I settle on the far side of the sea, even there Your hand will guide me, Your right hand will hold me fast."

– Psalm 139:9–10

"I will never leave you or forsake you."

– Hebrews 13:5

These aren't quaint metaphors. They're a spiritual reality.

You might feel alone, but you are not abandoned. You might feel distant, but you are not disconnected. God never needed a building to be near you. Again, the tearing of the Temple veil wasn't a symbolic gesture. The entire point of Pentecost was God declaring: *I'm not content with visiting you. I want to dwell in you.*

So, what does that mean in this wilderness season you're in? It means you don't have to claw your way back to God. He's already right beside you. It means you don't need to fake it until you "feel spiritual." You don't need a reset button, or a perfect repentance speech, or a clean record.

What you need is a fresh awareness.

Yes, you'll still have to deal with the hurt. You'll likely have old habits to break and deeply ingrained fears to unlearn. But none of that disqualifies you from God's nearness. In fact, it's the ground He uses to reveal Himself more intimately than you've ever known before.

So don't wait. Don't wait for the guilt to fade, or the perfect words, or the day you think you finally deserve it.

Just start by saying: *"God, I'm here."*

Because the whole time you thought He was silent, He's been whispering the same thing back: *"I'm here, too."*

Rediscovering Purpose Without Performance

What if the whole time you were scrambling to prove yourself, you were missing the point? What if your purpose was never supposed to be measured by how productive you could be?

Here's something you should know: When you leave the structures and schedules of church life, the questions start creeping in fast. (*"Now what am I supposed to do?"*) The programs, the ministries, the volunteer slots – they gave you something to hold onto, even when it felt performative or exhausting. At least there was a way to measure whether you were "spiritual enough." Show up, serve, tithe, smile, repeat. Simple. Predictable. Safe.

But once you're out of that cycle, it can feel like free fall.

Who are you when there's no title to cling to? No spiritual boss assigning you a task? No measuring stick to gauge whether you're doing it "right"?

I've got another hard truth for you: Much of what passes for discipleship has taught us that purpose equals performance. That God's approval is linked to how much you give, how hard you work, or how many people you serve. It's subtle. It sounds holy. But it's not the Kingdom Jesus preached.

> *"This is the work of God: that you believe in the One He has sent."*
> *– John 6:29*

Your primary assignment? It's not doing more. It's *abiding*.

And that word gets thrown around so much in church culture, it almost sounds passive. It isn't. Abiding means living with a constant awareness of God's presence. It means trusting Him in the tiny, unseen choices you make every day. It means letting your relationship with Him guide your responses instead of old scripts of obligation.

Abiding is not lazy. It's fiercely relational. It's how intimacy with God becomes the wellspring of your very being and your purpose. Instead of you constantly chasing His approval by doing more, you surrender to the transformation and molding He is working within you. You already have His approval, and you are becoming more... by His hand.

You don't earn purpose. You don't manufacture it. You *receive* it as a byproduct of walking with Him. And what does it look like? That's between you and Him.

When you're rooted in who God is and who you are to Him, what you're called to do flows naturally. Not as a compulsion, but as a Spirit-directed expression of love. And that looks different for everyone.

Sometimes it's resting – yes, rest can be an act of radical, Spirit-led obedience. Sometimes it's stepping out to create something, or to pour into others, or to open your door and offer quiet hospitality. Sometimes it's parenting with new patience. Sometimes it's showing up to your job with integrity in a world that celebrates shortcuts.

It shifts. It changes. There are seasons. That's what makes it real.

And you don't need a pulpit, a platform, or a polished resume to validate it. You don't need to prove its worth by numbers or applause.

"We are His workmanship, created in Christ Jesus for good works, which God prepared beforehand, that we should walk in them."

– Ephesians 2:10

Did you catch that? *Walk in them.* Not *strive* to build them. Not *stress* to measure up. Just... walk.

Your job isn't to make purpose happen. Your job is to stay connected with Him. Keep listening. Keep moving when He nudges you. The Spirit leads – you follow.

And in that rhythm, something new grows: A life that isn't shackled to obligation, but anchored in the freedom of love. You don't do it because you *have* to. You do it because you *get* to.

Learning to Walk With God In The Wild

There *is* life beyond the walls. But make no mistake – the terrain out here is wild and unfamiliar.

Walking away from religion isn't just stepping out of a building or laying down old doctrines. It's stepping into territory where the ground shifts under your feet. You've left behind the things you once leaned on – the programs, the pastors, the carefully scheduled sermons, the mission statements pinned up like signposts telling you where you're supposed to go next. And maybe you walked away because all that structure couldn't feed your soul anymore... but that doesn't make the wilderness any less intimidating.

What now? That question has a way of echoing in the empty spaces.

And let me tell you straight: There's no shame in asking it.

It's the same question the Israelites wrestled with when they stumbled out of Egypt, free but aimless, standing on scorched desert sand and realizing they didn't really know the God who brought them out. They had left bondage – but were they really heading somewhere better... or just lost?

You've left something that didn't work... but have you really entered something better?

Or are you just spiritually homeless?

The answer is: **It depends on what you do next.**

You're not in exile. You're in transition. You're not abandoned. You're just learning to follow a different kind of guide. You're not lost. You're learning to trust a different Voice.

And yes, the wild feels dangerous. Often, there are no signposts other than the quiet whisper of His Spirit. There's no safety net of human approval. No gold star attendance chart. It's unpredictable, threatening, messy... and holy. That's the point.

Out here, you don't get to follow a manmade program. You only get Him.

"See, I am doing a new thing! Now it springs up; do you not perceive it? I am making a way in the wilderness and streams in the wasteland."

– Isaiah 43:19

Do you see it? That's a promise.

In the wild, God isn't just beside you – He's speaking, leading, empowering you in ways that will change your life if you're willing to listen. Because when you stop orienting your faith around church programs or checking spiritual boxes, and you start building it around His *presence*, everything shifts.

This is where you learn to perceive the Spirit's nudges, see the small signs, feel the subtle stirrings that don't always fit neat theological categories. This is where relationship grows in place of ritual and religion.

It doesn't come instantly. It takes practice. It takes risk. It takes throwing out the old maps and believing, maybe for the first time, that the same God who spoke to prophets and disciples wants to speak to you, directly and personally.

The wilderness isn't a punishment. It's an invitation. It's where you go to unlearn old frameworks. A chance to let the Spirit retrain your heart and mind until His voice becomes more familiar than the noise that once surrounded you.

You weren't made to wander forever. You were made to *walk with God.*

So do that. Not on your terms. Not through anyone else's expectations. On *His* terms, in *His* voice, in the real, unpolished places of your everyday life.

You ready?

Then turn the page. Let's talk about how to hear Him for yourself.

Part III:

How To Converse With God

LEMOND PUBLISHING

About Part Three

When people learn to converse with God, everything changes.

This is something I've witnessed firsthand – not just in my own life but in the lives of others. I've seen people who once felt lost and disconnected experience a complete revival of their faith. I've watched destinies reignited, purpose restored, and lives transformed – all because they were willing to take a chance and dared to bring their questions to Him.

And while you may not believe this is possible for you just yet, let me assure you of one unshakable truth:

God always shows up.

Always.

It doesn't matter what you've done, how messy your past is, or what doubts or struggles you're wrestling with right now. God speaks to people who feel unworthy, to those who believe their mistakes define them, and even to people who don't believe in Him at all. I've seen Him speak to the hopeful and the hopeless, to believers and skeptics alike. I've seen Him break through the walls of the heartbroken, those who felt abandoned, overlooked, or forgotten by the world.

God always shows up. And when He does, He brings His unrelenting, overwhelming love and His gentle, transformative power.

But why?

Because God knows things about you that you don't yet know about yourself.

Your spirit came from God. And it's more than just the breath of life – it contains the image of the fully realized person He created you to be. Just as an oak tree is contained within the acorn, you are whole, complete, and made perfect in Him. But as an acorn needs soil, water, and time to grow into its potential, you need the nurturing presence of the Holy Spirit to mature into the fullness of the person God designed you to be.

This is why Christ went to the cross – to reconcile you back to the Father and to restore the relationship you were created for. Thanks to what Jesus accomplished, you have been made the very "righteousness of God." (**2 Corinthians 5:21**)

Everything that once separated you from His presence was removed. So if you're struggling to draw near to Him, it's not because you're unworthy; Christ already made you worthy. The real issue is that many believers fail to see their worth, or they allow fear and past wounds to hold them back from intimacy with God.

You are a **child of God**.

When you enter into the relationship Jesus died to give you, you belong to Him. Every promise of God, every provision of the Father, is available to you. His promises are more real, more certain, and more powerful than any circumstance or challenge you face – **but only if you accept them.**

- If you don't allow yourself the privilege of experiencing the depth of His love...

- If you hold on to the misguided idea that God is distant or unapproachable...

- If you fail to grasp that the cross permanently removed the stain of sin and made you clean before Him...

Then you won't realize who you are to Him.

This is why so many Christians struggle. They don't trust God because they don't truly know Him. And they don't know Him because they don't know themselves – their true spiritual identity as His children.

If you don't know who you are spiritually, you won't know how to develop intimacy with Him. Until you **recover and claim** your spiritual identity – the one God gave you – your faith will remain shallow. You'll find yourself drifting, a passive observer in this life rather than an active participant in your divine calling.

But you were created for so much more.

Your relationship with God isn't meant to be distant. You were created to walk in closeness with Him – to speak with Him, to hear from Him, and to know His heart just as He knows yours. This relationship is not optional; it is the very reason you were created.

God is not an angry judge waiting to condemn you. He is not an indifferent deity watching from afar. He is not the uninvolved God that religion has so often painted Him to be.

He is fully engaged. He is fully present. And He wants to be fully involved in every detail of your life.

Yet, far too many believers are leading lives of quiet desperation because they have never cultivated this kind of intimacy with the Holy Spirit. They have lost their sense of spiritual identity.

But here's the truth: **Christianity is not a self-improvement program.** It is not about trying harder, doing better, or checking off religious boxes in an attempt to become more righteous.

True transformation **only** comes through the Spirit.

That's why this process will work for you.

You don't need a particular religious background. You don't even need to believe that it will work for it to work. Skepticism, fear, doubt – bring them all with you.

All you need is a little curiosity. That's it. Turn off your inner critic for a moment and lean into the possibility that God is ready to speak directly to you.

Because I assure you... **He is.**

The question now is, "Are you?"

When you're ready, let's get started.

Chapter Fourteen

Your Mind, Your Words, Your Reality

To understand how God communicates with us, we first need to recognize how we are designed to connect with Him. This understanding is central to building a framework for conversation with God – a framework that I believe will transform your relationship with Him.

But let me tell you how I discovered this for myself.

Two years ago, I prayed for a practical way to help people build or deepen their personal, intimate relationship with God. While I've spent my life cultivating a close walk with Him, I found it challenging to help others find their way into that kind of intimacy.

Most of us are taught to talk *"AT"* God – presenting Him with a list of needs and desires – rather than to have a real, two-way conversation *"WITH"* Him. It was clear to me that what many people were missing wasn't faith, but connection.

I needed something simple and actionable that would guide people into that connection.

Just two days after that prayer, I happened to "stumble" across a man named Ed Rush speaking on a webinar. (I don't believe in coincidences, but I do believe in God's perfect timing.) I hadn't heard of Ed before, but within five minutes of listening to him, I knew he had something I'd been looking for. Right then and there, while the webinar was still running, I opened another tab on my computer and downloaded his book, **"God Talks: How to Have a Friendship With God (Even If You've Made a Million Mistakes)".**

I read the entire thing in a single day.

It was a revelation. Ed's framework was clear, approachable, and deeply resonant with everything I'd experienced in my own walk with God. He had managed to articulate something I'd known in my spirit but hadn't been able to put into words: A simple, practical process for connecting with God and hearing His voice.

Not four weeks later, although I wasn't prepared for it, God created the opportunity for me to attend one of Ed's early God Talks^{TM} Live events. I was excited to meet him in person, but what I found there went far beyond my expectations.

The community I encountered at that event was unlike anything I'd ever experienced. These were Kingdom-minded people, individuals driven by purpose and a desire to align their lives and businesses with God's will. They were there for something greater than themselves, and the atmosphere was alive with faith, freedom, and authenticity.

What stood out most was how this group of people were unhindered by a religious mindset. They weren't bound by the typical dogmas I have so often experienced that dominate church business settings. Instead, each person was focused on hearing directly from God for themselves. What really caught my attention was the fact that that focus created a powerful dynamic, a Spirit-led connection that permeated almost every conversation and interaction.

I can't fully describe in words what it felt like to be part of that event, but I can tell you it was real, transformative, and profoundly affecting. It reaffirmed what I already knew about what happens when people learn to converse with God: Lives change, barriers fall, purposes are reignited, and mountains get moved.

As a follower of Christ, I believe in these things. But this was remarkable to me in that I was seeing it happen before my eyes in a business environment. In my own career, I have been the beneficiary of what God can do when you partner with Him in business, but I'd never experienced it in the context of a cohesive community of individuals who were committed to conversing with God about their commercial enterprises.

I will tell you this: If you get the opportunity to attend a God Talks^{TM} Live event, don't miss it – whether you own a business or not.

Ed himself was as genuine and grounded as I had expected, and over time, he became more than a mentor; he became a friend. His guidance and the God Talks^{TM} framework have become a foundational part of my ministry and coaching. It's contributed to my own spiritual growth. Through this process, I've seen lives transformed, wounds healed, and destinies restored. And now, I want to share this process with you.

The Spirit Connection: How Your Mind Works

To understand how God communicates with us, we need to first understand how we are designed to connect with Him.

Science tells us that the mind has two primary parts: The **Conscious Mind**, which focuses on immediate tasks and logic, and the **Subconscious**

Mind, which processes problems, forms beliefs, and creates new pathways for learning.

But there's also a third part of the mind, what Ed calls the **Superconscious Mind**, and what I call "**your spirit**."

Your spirit is the unique part of you that connects directly with God. **Romans 8:16** says...

"The Spirit joins with our spirit to affirm that we are God's children."

— Romans 8:16

This connection isn't just figurative; it's real. The Holy Spirit entwines with your spirit to confirm your divine relationship and to restore the intimate connection God always intended for you to have.

Unfortunately, life has a way of interfering with this connection. Trauma, negative experiences, poor teaching, and even your own self-doubt can shut down the connection to God that Christ restored. However, this connection can be reopened in a matter of minutes. Once restored, the possibilities are endless. The Spirit of God will work with your spirit to renew your mind, heal your heart, and bring clarity and direction to your life.

Here's the incredible part: What could take years of effort and struggle can be resolved in moments when you're aligned with the Holy Spirit. Problems that seem insurmountable become manageable. Healing that feels impossible becomes reality. Transformation begins the moment you open yourself to His voice.

Words That Shape Your Life

The words we speak – whether aloud or in the quiet of our thoughts – are far more powerful than most people realize. Every word you say, intentionally or not, shapes the trajectory of your life. Words become the building blocks of your beliefs, your actions, and ultimately, your outcomes. What's more, these words don't just hover at the surface of your consciousness; they sink deep into your subconscious mind, where they create what Ed calls "contracts."

But before we delve into contracts, let's first unpack the relationship between the Conscious and Subconscious Minds, as understanding this dynamic is critical to fully grasping how your words influence your life.

Your Conscious Mind is where your focus resides. It's the part of your mind that gets things done. It handles your logical thinking, planning, decision-making, and processing... in the moment. You're using your Conscious Mind right now as you read this to analyze these words and decide what they mean to you.

Your Subconscious Mind, on the other hand, operates beneath the surface. It's the part of your mind responsible for identifying problems, finding solutions, and creating new neural pathways. Think of your subconscious as the "autopilot" system that manages the majority of your thoughts, behaviors, and reactions without your active awareness. It's always working in the background, guiding your habits, your emotions, and even your perceptions of the world. Most importantly, it operates based on the instructions it receives from your Conscious Mind – specifically, the words you use and the beliefs you hold.

How Contracts Affects You

Here's where contracts come in. A "contract" is like an internal agreement or belief that gets embedded into your Subconscious Mind. Once formed, it becomes a guiding force in your life, dictating how you perceive yourself, how you interact with others, and how you respond to the world around you.

Contracts are created by your Conscious Mind and are then sent to your Subconscious as instructions. They're formed by the words you tell yourself, whether positive or negative, and by the beliefs you adopt about your identity, your worth, and your circumstances.

For example, let's say you've faced rejection or failure in your life. You might begin to tell yourself, "I'm not good enough," or "I'll never succeed." Those words become a contract. Your Subconscious Mind processes those words as reality and begins to shape your thoughts, decisions, and actions to align with that belief. You start avoiding opportunities, doubting your abilities, or sabotaging your progress because your Subconscious Mind is working to fulfill the terms of the contract you've unknowingly written.

Negative Contracts vs. Positive Contracts

There are two types of contracts: Negative Contracts and Positive Contracts. Negative Contracts are formed when you internalize lies, fears, or limiting beliefs. They stem from negative life experiences, traumas, or harmful words spoken to you or by you.

For example:

- A parent says, "You'll never amount to anything," and the child internalizes that as truth.

- A teacher criticizes your efforts, and you adopt the belief, "I'm not smart enough."

- A series of failures leads you to tell yourself, "I'm a failure."

Each of these examples becomes a Negative Contract. And once that contract is embedded in your Subconscious, it becomes a self-fulfilling prophecy. You'll make decisions and take actions that align with the belief, even if it's not true.

But here's the good news: Positive Contracts can undo and replace Negative Contracts. Positive Contracts are formed when we internalize God's truth about who we are; truths that align with His Word and His promises. Positive Contracts originate from the Spirit of God, who speaks life, love, and purpose into us. They reshape how we see ourselves and the world.

For instance:

- The Negative Contract says, "I'm not good enough." The Positive Contract says, "I am fearfully and wonderfully made" (Psalm 139:14).

- The Negative Contract says, "I'll never succeed." The Positive Contract says, "I can do all things through Christ who strengthens me" (Philippians 4:13).

- The Negative Contract says, "I'm alone." The Positive Contract says, "God will never leave me nor forsake me" (Deuteronomy 31:6).

Why Words Matter

Here's the critical point: Contracts – whether negative or positive – are formed by words. Your words have the power to bind you to lies or free you with truth. Yet so few people understand the immense power of their words or the influence they have over their lives.

Think about the words you've spoken to yourself over the years. Are they words of hope, encouragement, and truth? Or are they words of doubt, fear, and limitation? If you've been telling yourself things like, "I'm not enough," "I'm a failure," or "Things will never change," you've been writing contracts that keep you stuck.

On the other hand, if you start speaking words of faith, love, and truth, words like, "God loves me," "I am capable," or "I can trust God's plan for my life," you'll begin writing Positive Contracts that align your Subconscious Mind with God's truth. And when your Subconscious Mind is aligned with God's truth, everything changes.

How Positive Contracts Overcome Negative Ones

One beauty of God's design is that Negative Contracts can be broken. Through the guidance of the Holy Spirit, you can identify the lies you've believed, replace them with God's truth, and recode your mind with Positive Contracts.

If you've been living under the Negative Contract, "I am alone," through the God Talks™ process, you bring this lie to God, and He reveals the truth: "You are never alone. I have always been with you, and I always will be." That truth becomes your new Positive Contract: "I am never alone. God is with me, always."

As you affirm divine truth by speaking it, writing it, and meditating on it, you reprogram your Subconscious Mind. Old Negative Contracts lose their power, and new Positive Contracts take root. These new and greater truths shape your thoughts, your actions, and your reality.

Your Words Shape Your World

Your words are not just sounds or fleeting thoughts; they are the building blocks of your natural life and existence. They shape your beliefs, your actions, and your destiny. **Proverbs 18:21** reminds us, **"The tongue has the power of life and death."** The words you speak – to yourself and others – have the power to create life or destroy it.

If you want to change your life, start by changing your words. Speak truth, speak life, and speak God's promises over yourself. And when you do, the contracts in your mind begin to shift. Negative Contracts lose their grip, and Positive Contracts take root. This is the beginning of how the Holy Spirit transforms you from the inside out.

The power of your words is a reflection of the power of God's Word. And when you align your words with His truth, there is no limit to what He can do in and through you. Let this be the day you begin to speak life, rewrite your contracts, and step into the fullness of who God created you to be.

Now that you know all this, you can undo all of your Negative Contracts, replace them with Positive Contracts, and change your world by changing your words. And the fastest, easiest way to do that is by replacing your old words with the Words God has for you.

The only thing left is for me to show you how to connect to God to develop a dialog so that you can ask and get answers to receive the powerful words He has for you.

Now it's about to get real.

Chapter Fifteen

A Framework for Conversing With God

It's time to drop your human defenses and turn on your spiritual curiosity. I'm about to teach you a straightforward process that has changed tens of thousands of lives and will change yours, too. I'm merely going to reintroduce you to God and then get out of the way. He'll do the rest.

The Process: A Dialogue With God

The God Talks™ framework is simple but profound, consisting of three key steps:

1. **Preparing Your Mind** - This step involves quieting the noise of your Conscious Mind so you can listen with your spirit. You'll use techniques like focused breathing and intentional prayer to center yourself and invite God to speak. **(10 minutes)**

2. **Asking God Two Questions** - These questions are designed to uncover the negative beliefs that hold you back and reveal the truth that God wants you to embrace. **(5 minutes)**

3. **Recode Your Mind With Two Statements** - Using what you've heard from God, you'll create two powerful statements: *"I let go of the lie that..."* and *"I receive the truth that..."* These statements will help you replace old, harmful beliefs with new, life-giving truths from God. **(5 minutes or as long as it takes to sink in)**

So as you can see, starting out, you'll want to set aside at least 20 minutes for your God Talks™ exercises.

That said, until you've gotten used to it, it's not unusual for some people to take up to 20 minutes to get into "resonance" (or get "in the zone," as others like to say) with Step 1 to hear from God before asking the Two Questions.

If it takes you a little longer, that's fine. It gets faster with practice. These days, I can prepare my mind in about a minute and complete the entire process in less than three. (I usually prefer to take longer, though.) It's just about practice and consistency.

Don't worry about the time. Any time you give directly to God will be given back to you in multitudes. If you don't understand that now, it's okay. You will. You're on the verge of learning a lot of things about God you didn't know before.

Again, you don't have to have any particular religious belief system for this process to work. You don't even have to believe that it will work for it to work. If you're a little nervous, a little scared, or even a lot skeptical, it's okay.

Just be curious. Turn off your inner critic. Take a chance that this will turn out for good because it will.

In a few minutes, as part of this audio, I'm going to walk you through a guided God Talks™ exercise. You don't have to go at this alone.

But before we get started with that, let me describe the process in depth.

STEP #1: PREPARE YOUR MIND.

When I ask people to close their eyes and prepare to connect with God, they often tell me the same thing: As soon as they do, their thoughts start running wild, and they can't focus. Sound familiar? That's normal, and it happens for a reason.

Think of your Conscious Mind as a monkey swinging from branch to branch. It's constantly jumping around from one thought to the next, and the moment you give it space, it starts delivering reminders and to-do lists you've probably been ignoring.

These distractions might sound like:

- Don't forget to pick up the groceries.

- What am I going to wear to the meeting tomorrow?

- I need to schedule that dentist appointment I've been putting off.

- Did I respond to that email yet?

This mental "noise" is just part of freeing up your mind, so don't worry. It's completely normal. The key is to approach it with patience and grace, not frustration. Trust the process – this is the beginning of preparing your mind to connect with God.

Why This Works

The God Talks™ process isn't magic; it's rooted in how God designed your mind and spirit. When you align your spirit with His Spirit, you open the door to clarity, healing, transformation, and divine communication.

This process is not about striving or trying harder. It's about stepping into the relationship God has already prepared for you. It's about allowing Him to do the work of renewal and transformation in your life. As you begin to hear His voice and receive His truth, you'll discover a freedom, joy, and purpose that only come from walking in alignment with Him.

Your Next Step

Now it's time to take a step of faith. Find a quiet space to give this process a try. You don't have to get it perfect, and you won't be doing it alone. I'll guide you through the steps, but ultimately, this is about you and God.

Now it's time to prepare your mind and take a step of faith. Find a quiet, comfortable space where you can focus without distractions. Once you're ready it should take about 10 minutes. Here's what you'll need to do:

1. **Grab a Pen and Paper.** I find it best to use something simple like a journal or a yellow pad, but anything you can write on will do. I don't recommend you use your phone, tablet, or computer. Technology brings too many distractions. If you're using your phone for the audios, be sure to put it in Airplane Mode. You need to be fully present and undistracted. .

2. **Settle In.** Find a comfortable place to sit. Take a few deep breaths and let yourself relax.

3. **Breathe and Focus.** Close your eyes. Slowly breathe in through your nose and out through your nose, focusing your attention on the air moving in and out. Let go of everything else. If a random thought pops up (and one or more probably will) – like something you need or forgot to do – simply write it down, then close your eyes and return to your breathing. Quietly tune out

distractions and allow your mind to rest. This gets easier the more you practice it.

4. **Invite God to Speak.** As part of preparing your mind, start with a short prayer or invitation for God to join you. It doesn't have to be formal or perfect; just speak from your heart. Here's an example:

"God, thank You for being here. Thank You for joining me in this process. Right now, I invite You to speak while I listen. I choose to hear from You and You alone. Amen."

You can speak this prayer just as it is, but feel perfectly free to use your own words. There's nothing special about the way words need to be put together. (In fact, you should always talk to God in a way that is most natural and comfortable for you. Despite what many have been taught, He doesn't stand on ceremony or formalities.)

Before you begin the process, always take a moment to intentionally invite Him into this time. Just ask Him to speak. Set your intention to listen. I find the short invitation above helps to center your mind and prepare your spirit to connect with the Holy Spirit.

In the audio exercises that follow, I'll guide you with specific breathing techniques accompanied by music to help slow you down and settle into Heaven's pace so you can listen. I think it's more effective to use the audios when you're getting started, but doing it yourself is fine, if that's what you prefer.

Once you feel ready, go on to...

STEP #2: ASK GOD THE TWO QUESTIONS.

This is where things get exciting. You'll likely experience something that's completely new and different. Prepare yourself for the unexpected. Hearing from God directly is unlike anything else. He speaks to each of us in unique ways, but I promise you this: He will show up for you.

You're going to ask God two very specific, very important questions to start.

Ask the First Question: *"What lies do I believe about myself?"*

Close your eyes. Be still and calm. Be aware of your breath. Focus on God and receiving from Him and Him alone.

Then, write down whatever you hear, see, sense, or feel – **without editing**. Those last two words are emphasized for a purpose. Don't second-guess what you're writing. I repeat, write down whatever you hear, see, sense, or feel – **WITHOUT EDITING**. Just let it flow. If you smell something, write it down. If you hear a random word, write it down. If you see a mental image, write it down. Whatever it is, don't edit it, don't overanalyze, or filter it. Just write everything down.

Trust the process.

Here's why: God often communicates in ways that might not make sense at first. He speaks to your spirit in ways that are deeply personal, and sometimes those messages unfold over time. Don't be surprised if what you write seems puzzling now but clicks later. He works in mysterious and meaningful ways.

Take your time. Don't be in a hurry. Only once you've written down everything that you've been impressed with, continue on with the second question.

Ask God the Second Question *"God, What is true about me?"*

Again, write down everything that comes to you, without editing. God may reveal truths about your identity, your worth, or His love for you. These truths are treasures. Capture them as they come, even if they feel overwhelming or hard to believe at first.

Write everything down... WITHOUT EDITING.

God knows more about you than you know about yourself. This step is about uncovering the lies you've been carrying and replacing them with His truth. This peels back layers of false belief and further uncovers your true spiritual identity. Trust me, this is information you need.

Once you've asked both questions and recorded your responses, it's time to move on to the final step.

STEP #3: RECODE YOUR MIND WITH TWO STATEMENTS.

This step is vital. While Step #2 reveals the lies and truths, Step #3 is where transformation begins. It's not enough to hear God's truth. You need to take it and recode your Subconscious Mind with it. This is how you break free from the negative contracts that have been holding you back.

Think about it this way: Step #2 is the diagnosis, and Step #3 is the cure. It doesn't make sense to go to the doctor, get a diagnosis, and then do nothing about it. The diagnosis is just information.

It won't do you any good to hear a new truth about yourself and then not recode your Subconscious Mind. So in Step #3, you will take what you heard from God and use your Conscious Mind to recode your Subconscious with a new Positive Contract.

Here's how it works:

1. **Let Go of the Lies:** Take each lie you identified in Step #2 and

create a statement to release it. You take the lies from Step #1 and word them into a sentence like this: "I let go of the lie that (_____)."

2. **Receive the Truth:** Take each truth you heard and create a statement to accept it. Then, take what's true and insert it into the sentence... "I receive (_____)."

Speak these statements out loud. Use your voice and your body. Get physical. Make motions. Push your hands away from your body when you let go of lies. Place your hands over your heart when you receive the truths. This physical engagement reinforces the new coding in your Subconscious Mind. Don't hold back. This is your time to claim freedom and truth.

Repeat for each and every lie.

The following is an example from Ed's book, "**God Talks.**"

Maia heard the following lies:

- *"You are unworthy."*

- *"You are ugly."*

- *"You don't mean anything to Me."*

But when she asked what was true, God revealed:

- *"You are worthy."*

- *"You are beautiful."*

- *"I love you just the way I made you."*

Maia's statements for Step #3 looked like this:

- *"I let go of the lie that I am unworthy."*

- *"I receive that I am worthy."*

- *"I let go of the lie that I am ugly."*

- *"I receive that I am beautiful."*

- *"I let go of the lie that I don't mean anything to God."*

- *"I receive that God loves me just the way He made me."*

The bottom line is to take what you learned in Step #2 and use it in a new Subconscious coding for Step #3.

Now it's your turn to let go of the lies and receive God's truth. Remember, this is a process. You don't have to get it perfect. The most important thing is to be open and willing. God is faithful to meet you right where you are.

So, let's get started. I'll walk you through the first of Ed's "God Talks" exercises myself. I don't think I'm as good as Ed, but you'll get the gist and still benefit from the process. You'll experience the power of hearing directly from your Creator. This is the beginning of a life-changing journey. God's truth has the power to set you free. Don't trust me, trust Him.

For exercise two, follow the exact same process except replace the two questions with these two:

1. **Ask the First Question:** *"God, what lies do I believe about you?"*

2. **Ask the Second Question:** *"God, what is true about you that I need to know today?"*

Even if it doesn't feel like it's working at first, keep at it until you break through. Repeat the full process as often as you need to. God Talks™ is about God Himself talking, and I assure you He's ready to chat with you. Your challenge is to learn how to listen.

If you don't give up, you will not fail.

And you will find freedom.

You have a greater mission in life than you know, but first, you need to change your words, to change your thoughts, to change your actions. And there are no better words than those that God will give you.

Go ahead and get started. If you're listening to the audiobook version of this book, these exercises follow. Otherwise, (or in addition to), you can download the audio exercises I've prepared for you by typing the URL for each one into any device or computer:

Get AUDIO EXERCISE #1 here: https://dge4.me/audio1

Audio Exercise 1

Get AUDIO EXERCISE #2 here: https://dge4.me/audio2

Audio Exercise 2

Follow-up

Congratulations again on completing the two audio exercises. I'd love to hear from you on what they did for you and where you're going from here.

When you purchase Ed's book (and I strongly recommend that you do), he provides you with seven audios that guide you through key topics – a full week's worth.

Ed's guided audio exercises are a wonderful place to start in learning how to dialogue with God as well as powerful daily practices for cultivating a direct relationship with Him. That's why I use them in my coaching. I also create audio exercises for my clients. I see the results that people get with this framework. It's nothing less than extraordinary because when people finally know the truth about themselves and God, they get straight about their past, future, and a whole lot more.

Even if it feels awkward at first or doesn't feel like it's working, keep at it until you break through. Repeat the process as often as you need to. These aren't "one and done" exercises. God Talks™ is about God Himself talking to you and you becoming proficient in listening and attuning yourself to His voice.

If you don't give up, you will not fail. Again, I recommend purchasing the God Talks™ book to learn more, and with it, you'll receive Ed's other audios. You can also inquire about joining the "God Talks" online community or even my group coaching program. With either, you'll get additional "God Talks^{TM}" audio exercises.

As Ed would say, "Give it a shot. Then keep at it. Failure is not an option."

This does work and will work for you.

Part IV:

Healing & Moving Forward

LEMOND PUBLISHING

Chapter Sixteen

Understanding The Source of Pain

N ow we get down to it.

The wounds inflicted by toxic church environments run deep. Church-hurt is something they are all too familiar with, and yet it's something that few churches are equipped to address openly. The very environment meant to offer sanctuary, love, and spiritual nourishment has, for countless individuals, become a source of pain, betrayal, and confusion.

If this has been your experience, I'm sorry. You're not alone, and your pain is valid.

In my experience, most of the pain and hurt people experience in churches occurs precisely because they have not been taught to keep church in its proper perspective. When you elevate the institution to a place of ultimate authority, you risk disappointment, disillusionment, and even spiritual wounds, especially when the people in these institutions fail or act out of alignment with God's will.

Fortunately, the quickest and easiest way to overcome this kind of pain, heal, and move forward in confidence and purpose is to realign your beliefs and place the Holy Spirit in His proper position in your life. He alone is meant to be your ultimate guide and teacher.

Why People Get Hurt By Church

Churches, like any human institution, are imperfect. Despite their best intentions, they can fall short of God's calling. But the truth is, when we place our faith in the institution rather than directly in God, we set ourselves up for disappointment and hurt.

That said, the circumstances surrounding Church-hurt are as diverse as the people who experience it, but they often stem from a few unfortunate but common circumstances. Let's reexamine the stories of Shelia, Karen, and Thomas as examples:

1. Misplaced Trust in Institutions

For many believers, the church becomes far more than just a gathering space. It becomes the centerpiece of their faith journey – the place where they learn about God, find community, and seek spiritual nourishment. But there's a quiet danger in giving the institution itself ultimate authority in your spiritual life. When we trust the church more than who the church was meant to point us toward, disappointment becomes inevitable.

Remember Sheila's story? She grew up in a tight-knit congregation that felt like home. The rituals, the traditions, the routine of showing up week after week – it all seemed holy, meaningful, a sure sign that she was on the right path. But over the years, as life's hard questions emerged, Sheila found the church's answers to be rote and shallow. She began to feel the disconnect between the vibrant God she read about in Scripture and the institution that seemed more concerned with preserving tradition than engaging with the living Spirit. When she dared to voice her questions, to suggest that maybe there was something missing beneath all the rituals, she found herself subtly shut out. Sideways glances. Polite smiles that didn't reach the eyes. Gossip whispered just loud enough for her to hear. The place that had once been home became cold, unfamiliar, and she wondered where exactly she'd gone wrong.

The painful truth is, churches are made up of people. And people, however well-intentioned, are fallible. They fail. They fall short. They cling to comfort and tradition. And when we place our trust in the system rather than in the God who breathed life into us, the cracks will show. The betrayal cuts deep precisely because we elevated something human to a place only God deserves. That pain is real, but it can also be the invitation to shift your trust back where it belongs.

"Do not put your trust in princes, in human beings, who cannot save."

— Psalm 146:3

2. Toxic Leadership and Control

The church was never meant to be a place where power is hoarded, where leaders elevate themselves at the expense of those they serve. Jesus made that crystal clear. But too often, leadership structures become hierarchical fortresses – places where authority matters more than humility, where numbers and programs take precedence over the messy work of genuine care.

If Shelia's story resonates with you, know that perhaps even more people relate to Karen's. Her church looked picture-perfect on the outside: Modern building, polished worship team, friendly greeters. But behind the smiles, Karen felt unseen. Leadership in her church talked about outreach and love, but they measured success by attendance charts and social media metrics. If you had questions or doubts, there wasn't space for that – you were quietly shuffled into a program, given a book to read, or brushed off with spiritual jargon.

Karen longed for a place where she could share her real struggles, where someone would just sit with her in the mess. Instead, she felt like a statistic in someone else's success story – a tool for the leadership's vision, rather than a beloved child of God.

Jesus warned about this kind of spiritual hierarchy. He didn't mince words.

*"**You know that the rulers of the Gentiles lord it over them, and their high officials exercise authority over them. Not so with you. Instead, whoever wants to become great among you must be your servant.**"*

– Matthew 20:25-26

When leaders forget that they are called to serve – not control – the result is a culture of quiet fear. People become objects to be managed rather than hearts to be shepherded. And that leaves wounds that often take years to unearth and heal.

3. LEGALISM AND PERFORMANCE-BASED FAITH

Legalism is one of the most pervasive sources of church-inflicted pain. It creeps in subtly, disguised as spiritual discipline, commitment, or "holiness." But underneath the language of obedience is a dark undercurrent: Perform, or you are unworthy. Measure up, or be cast out. Look the part, check the boxes, never let your flaws show – and maybe, just maybe, you'll be accepted.

Churches that emphasize strict adherence to rules and outward behavior over inward transformation create an environment where love and grace are conditional. Such policies and false beliefs lead people back into the very cycle of striving and self-effort that Christ put an end to. While this approach may be well-intentioned, it is misguided and actively works against the freedom He restored to us. It creates barriers and makes people feel unfit and distant from God when they fail to measure up to church standards. Believers are left feeling burdened, inadequate, and perpetually unworthy.

As we've seen, however, under the New Covenant, God's love and acceptance are freely given, not earned through performance or perfection.

Thomas learned his lesson the hard way. He grew up in a church steeped in tradition, where the unspoken rule was that you kept your doubts to yourself and maintained appearances at all costs. The sermons rarely addressed the real, daily challenges Thomas was facing. Instead, they hammered home moral standards and pious clichés.

Over time, Thomas felt like he was wearing a mask – saying the right things, doing the right things, but hollow on the inside. The church preached grace, but in practice, grace was always conditional, measured against performance and compliance. Eventually, Thomas burned out.

The rituals that once gave structure to his faith became a prison that kept him from a real relationship with God.

Legalism reduces faith to a set of rules to follow rather than a relationship with God to nurture. It replaces the freedom of the New Covenant with the burdens of the old, leaving believers feeling trapped and disconnected. Legalism takes the gospel – the good news that we are saved by grace alone – and twists it into a treadmill of human effort. But Paul reminded us:

> *"For it is by grace you have been saved, through faith – and this is not from yourselves, it is the gift of God – not by works, so that no one can boast."*
>
> *– Ephesians 2:8-9*

If you've been caught in that cycle, hear me: It's not of God. And you don't have to stay there.

4. LACK OF GENUINE COMMUNITY

Perhaps one of the deepest wounds comes not from overt abuse or harsh leadership, but from the quiet ache of loneliness in the very place that promised family. Churches often talk about community. They build programs, small groups, events, and more, but too often, it stays at the surface. Polite smiles. Warm handshakes. The "How are you?" greetings that never wait for an honest answer.

One of the most painful aspects of Church-hurt is the absence of authentic relationships. Churches may emphasize programs and activities but fail to foster genuine connections. Believers may find themselves surrounded by people yet feeling profoundly alone.

Community is the heart of the Body of Christ, where believers support one another, share burdens, and grow together in faith. When true community is missing, it leaves a void that no amount of church programming can fill.

But true community is messy. It requires vulnerability, patience, grace, and the willingness to sit with someone in their doubt and fear without fixing them. It requires making space for differences, for grief, for raw humanity.

I've listened to more stories of believers who showed up hoping to be known – hoping that maybe, this time, they'd find real friends, a spiritual family who would walk with them no matter how ugly or complicated life got. And too often, they left feeling more alone than when they came in. That emptiness can be devastating.

Scripture calls us to something deeper:

Beloved, let us love one another, because love comes from God. Everyone who loves has been born of God and knows God. Whoever does not love does not know God, because God is love.

– 1 John 4:7-8

"Carry each other's burdens, and in this way you will fulfill the law of Christ."

– Galatians 6:2

If you've experienced the ache of being unseen in church, know this: It wasn't supposed to be that way. And the longing you carry for genuine community? That is holy. It echoes God's own heart for His people.

Steps to Healing from Church Wounds

Healing from the wounds you've experienced in church isn't a quick fix. It's a journey that God longs to walk with you step by step. Your pain is real, and it matters. But it doesn't have to define your faith or your relationship with Him. Here are some steps you can take to move toward healing, restoration, and renewed confidence in who God is to you.

1. ACKNOWLEDGE THE PAIN

You can't heal what you won't admit. That's not weakness – that's courage. The first step in healing is to be honest about the hurt you've experienced. Maybe it was the sting of judgment from people who were supposed to love you. Maybe it was leaders who failed you, or a community that turned their backs when you needed them most, or possibly the slow drip of legalism and performance that hollowed out your joy. Whatever it was, ignoring it or pushing it down will only let the wound fester and deepen.

Bring it into the light. Name it. Let yourself feel the grief and the anger and the confusion. Tell God exactly how you feel – He can handle it. And remember:

"The Lord is close to the brokenhearted and saves those who are crushed in spirit."

– Psalm 34:18

2. FORGIVE THOSE WHO HURT YOU

Nothing about this is easy. Forgiveness isn't about pretending what happened was okay. It isn't about letting others off the hook or ignoring the damage done. Forgiveness is about freeing yourself from the heavy chains of bitterness. It's about refusing to let the past control your heart, your thoughts, or your future.

What is most important to understand is that forgiveness doesn't start with you trying to conjure it up through gritted teeth. It starts with God. His forgiveness flows *to* you and *through* you. It's a gift that releases you from resentment and opens your heart to healing and restoration.

> *"Bear with each other and forgive one another if any of you has a grievance against someone. Forgive as the Lord forgave you."*
> — *Colossians 3:13*

3. REALIGN YOUR FAITH WITH GOD

There's every chance that the pain you've experienced happened because you anchored your faith in a system – a charismatic leader, a group of people, a polished program – rather than with the God those people and things were meant to point you toward.

It's a subtle shift, but it makes all the difference.

Now is the time to place God back where He belongs: At the center. Shift your trust away from flawed human structures and fix your eyes on

Him. Let Him be your rock, your source, your foundation that cannot be shaken. He is the one who never changes and never fails.

"Trust in the Lord with all your heart and lean not on your own understanding; in all your ways submit to him, and he will make your paths straight."

— Proverbs 3:5-6

4. SEEK THE HOLY SPIRIT'S GUIDANCE

You don't have to figure this out alone. You were never meant to. Jesus called the Holy Spirit the Comforter, the Counselor, and the Guide. He leads you into truth, restores what was broken, and brings peace where there was chaos.

Ask the Spirit to reveal the places in your heart that need healing. Let Him highlight where bitterness and hurt still linger. Trust Him to show you how to move forward – not in human wisdom, but in His wisdom, helping you discern God's will and restoring your relationship with Him. Through the Holy Spirit, you experience the peace, joy, and transformation that only God can provide.

"But the Advocate, the Holy Spirit, whom the Father will send in my name, will teach you all things and will remind you of everything I have said to you."

— John 14:26

5. CULTIVATE A DIRECT RELATIONSHIP WITH GOD

This is not only the heartbeat of healing, it's also the key to kingdom living: Building your own, intimate relationship with God that isn't mediated through an institution or measured by how well you perform. God wants you – *your real, disordered, questioning, searching self* – in direct, daily relationship. Develop daily practices of conversation that nurture and expand your direct connection with Him.

This isn't about checking off spiritual tasks to prove you're faithful. It's about lingering in conversation with Him, letting Him speak into your everyday moments, and learning to hear His voice for yourself. Let Him shape how you read Scripture, how you live your faith, how you see yourself.

> *"Remain in me, as I also remain in you. No branch can bear fruit by itself; it must remain in the vine. Neither can you bear fruit unless you remain in me."*
>
> *– John 15:4*

Moving Forward in Freedom

You are not defined by what was done to you in the past. Your faith is not bound by human structures or limited by the wounds you've carried. Your faith is rooted in the unchanging love of God, in the Spirit that transforms and makes you new, and in the One who calls you His own.

As you walk this path of healing, remember: God is leading you into deeper relationship with Him. He is restoring your confidence, your trust, your purpose. He is freeing you from bitterness and fear, giving you new eyes to see, new ears to hear, and a new heart to love others out of the overflow of His love for you.

Thriving in intimacy with God isn't about perfect church attendance, polished theology, or flawless spiritual routines. It's about letting His Spirit guide you every day. It's about learning how to live as someone deeply loved and forgiven, who carries the Kingdom inside them into a hurting world.

The abundant life you were created for – the one Jesus promised – is not a list of religious tasks to complete. It is a life of love, purpose, and joy, walking every day beside the One who made you.

So trust Him. Let Him lead you into that life.

Now is the time to embrace it fully.

Chapter Seventeen

The Importance of Community

I t's important to heal from past wounds, to unlearn harmful patterns, to let the Holy Spirit breathe life into the dry places of your soul. But that's not where the journey ends. God never designed you to walk this road alone – not then, not now. As important as it is to face the pain and break free from toxic structures, it's just as crucial to rediscover the life-giving gift of true spiritual community.

Don't let the hurts of the past convince you that isolation is safer, or holier, or somehow more spiritual. God created us for connection – real, messy, Spirit-led connection. That might mean finding a new church. It might mean gathering in a home fellowship, or meeting in a living room with a handful of friends, praying and sharing a meal, singing songs and praises, lifting each other up when the world tries to tear us down.

Whatever form it takes, community is not optional. It's essential.

The writer of Hebrews knew this when he urged:

"And let us consider how we may spur one another on toward love and good deeds, not giving up meeting together, as some are in the

habit of doing, but encouraging one another — and all the more as you see the Day approaching."

— Hebrews 10:24-25

The early believers understood this in a way we often forget. They didn't call themselves "the Church." They were called the Ekklesia – the called-out ones. They were not bound to buildings or tied to rituals. Their gatherings were organic, simple, and alive. The book of Acts tells us they met daily in the temple courts – open spaces where anyone could join – but also in homes, breaking bread, praying, and sharing their lives and testimonies. Their faith was rooted in shared dependence on the Holy Spirit and each other. And God blessed them.

"Every day they continued to meet together in the temple courts. They broke bread in their homes and ate together with glad and sincere hearts, praising God and enjoying the favor of all the people. And the Lord added to their number daily those who were being saved."

— Acts 2:46-47

When persecution came, when the temple was destroyed and the world turned against them, they kept meeting in homes. They gathered around kitchen tables and in back rooms, carrying each other's burdens, celebrating victories, sitting together in grief and joy alike. They didn't need a polished stage to make God show up. They just needed each other and the Spirit that bound them together.

Similar acts are increasingly breaking out today, as well. A handful of believers in a living room, sharing food and stories of God's faithfulness. No formalities, just raw hunger for God and the freedom to be real. I've met with friends gathering under trees in a park, strumming guitars, praying over each other, laughing and crying in the same breath. This is the Ekklesia. This is the Body.

Let me be clear: I'm not here to bash church attendance. God can and does work powerfully in many traditional congregations. But don't let anyone convince you that the institution is the most important thing. Your primary focus needs to be on following the leading of the Holy Spirit, relationship with one another, and the shared commitment to seeking God together.

You mustn't allow past wounds to lock you away from the gift of community. Whether it's a home group, a Spirit-led congregation, or something that doesn't fit neatly in any box, God wants you connected to others of the Body of Christ.

Doing so may not always be easy. Over the course of my life, I've been part of churches that drained the life out of me – places where programs and politics smothered the Spirit, where leaders built kingdoms of their own rather than tending God's flock. But I've also been blessed to belong to churches that stoked the fire in my soul, where the Spirit's presence wasn't just felt during worship, but guided every decision leaders made.

That's the difference. It's easy to find churches where the Spirit is present – you can sense Him in the music, in the emotion of the congregation. But Spirit-led churches? In my experience, those are rare. Those are the places where leaders humble themselves before the Spirit's whisper, where decisions are made not by strategy but by surrender. Where the Spirit leads from the top down and transforms everything from the way people are welcomed at the door to how the congregation engages the community.

How can you tell? Ask God to guide you. He will. My wife and I have made it a practice not to join congregations where the Lord doesn't lead us. I didn't always do that, and let's just say the results were poor.

(BTW, visiting doesn't count. I've attended many churches of different denominations and religious traditions, where God directed me, if only to let His light shine or be a blessing to others.)

Spirit-led churches bear fruit. They overflow with love, grace, and radical generosity. They aren't perfect, but they're alive. And they prove what the early Ekklesia already knew: The Kingdom of Heaven isn't built on programs or platforms, but on people surrendered to the Spirit of God, bound together by love, and committed to carrying one another through the mess and the miracle of following Jesus.

Leading Without Hierarchy

These days, one of the most overlooked realities of the early Ekklesia was its lack of rigid, human-constructed hierarchies. Unlike the towering institutional structures many of us have experienced, where a select few hold authority over the many, the New Testament model offers something beautifully countercultural: A community led by the Spirit, where leadership exists to serve rather than to dominate.

Paul lays this out plainly in his letter to the Ephesians:

"So Christ himself gave the apostles, the prophets, the evangelists, the pastors and teachers, to equip his people for works of service, so that the body of Christ may be built up until we all reach unity in the faith and in the knowledge of the Son of God and become mature, attaining to the whole measure of the fullness of Christ."

– Ephesians 4:11-13

Notice what Paul doesn't say: That these roles exist to set certain people above the rest, or to create layers of power and control. Instead, these roles are given so the *entire body* can be equipped, so *everyone* can grow into maturity and walk in the fullness of Christ. That's the point. Leadership in the Kingdom isn't about status, it's about *service*. It's not about consolidating power, but about releasing it, multiplying it, spreading it among the people of God. The Ekklesia is a living, breathing, Spirit-led movement – not a machine with cogs and gears and top-down control.

Of course, this doesn't mean there's no order. Even in a Spirit-led community, someone has to facilitate, organize, and do the work. We hold each other accountable. But true authority in the Body of Christ always flows from the Holy Spirit first. And when leaders submit themselves fully to His direction, the community becomes a place of collaborative discernment, mutual respect, and shared growth. No one is greater or lesser. We are all co-laborers, each bringing a piece of the puzzle, each indispensable to the whole.

Does that mean hierarchy is inherently evil? No. Human organizations require structure. Someone must keep the books, ensure decisions are made, and serve those in need. But the ultimate authority you answer to is not the person with the biggest title or the flashiest platform – it's God Himself. A healthy spiritual community never loses sight of that.

Authentic Worship

If you've been in church long enough, you've heard hundreds of messages on worship. You've likely experienced stirring music, emotional altar calls, maybe even moments that felt transcendent in the sanctuary. But all too often, our idea of worship gets confined to those moments – those events, those services, those familiar songs.

Jesus shattered that box in one conversation with a Samaritan woman at a well.

"A time is coming and has now come when the true worshipers will worship the Father in the Spirit and in truth, for they are the kind of worshipers the Father seeks."

– John 4:23

Worship isn't about the right location, the right liturgy, or the perfect song set. It isn't about following a formula. True worship is about the heart – your heart seeking God in Spirit and truth, without pretense, fear, or agenda.

And that means worship can happen anywhere. It can be in a living room, with voices lifted in imperfect harmony. It can be alone in your car, tears streaming as you thank God for His goodness. It can be in the quiet moment when you hold the hand of someone hurting, choosing to serve in Jesus' name. Worship isn't an event. It's a *life*. It's the way we live in constant awareness of God's presence, the way we respond to His goodness with gratitude, surrender, and praise.

This is what the Ekklesia was – and is – meant to be. A community unshackled by tradition, unhindered by walls. A gathering of Spirit-led people, seeking God together, loving one another deeply, growing in grace and truth, and pouring themselves out in acts of worship that spill far beyond any church service.

When you surrender leadership to God, serve lovingly, gather meaningfully, and worship authentically, you will taste what it truly means to be the Body of Christ – a living temple where His Spirit moves freely, and where every believer is empowered to step into the fullness of an abundant life. That's not just a vision. That's what Jesus meant when He called us out to be His people.

Your Spiritual Community: Worship, Service, & Living Faith Together

As you continue this journey, take a moment to thoughtfully consider what your spiritual community looks like – or what you hope it will look like in the days ahead. The early Ekklesia offers a stunning blueprint for what the Body of Christ can be: A gathering of believers bound not by walls or rituals, but by shared purpose, authentic worship, and a radical, Spirit-led commitment to love.

Community isn't confined to a building or an institution. It's not about flashy programs or carefully scripted services. True community happens in living rooms and around kitchen tables. It happens in backyards, in parks, in quiet conversations over coffee. It happens wherever believers gather meaningfully, seeking God in Spirit and truth, just as Jesus described.

In a real Ekklesia, leadership isn't about rank, titles, or control. It's about Spirit-led collaboration, where each person brings their gifts to build up the Body. It's about serving others in love, stepping into the mess and the beauty of life with a commitment to generosity, compassion, and grace. Worship in this kind of community isn't limited to Sunday mornings – it becomes a way of life. Every act of kindness, every word of encouragement, every meal shared in His name is an act of worship. It's living out your faith with integrity, rooted in gratitude for all He's done.

Jesus put it simply:

"By this everyone will know that you are my disciples, if you love one another."

— John 13:35

That type of love doesn't stay inside the circle. A Spirit-led community is never just inward-focused – it's always looking outward, finding ways to serve, to lift burdens, to bring hope and light into dark places. As Paul wrote:

"You, my brothers and sisters, were called to be free. But do not use your freedom to indulge the flesh; rather, serve one another humbly in love."

— Galatians 5:13

This is more than charity. Service is worship in action – the gospel made visible. It's feeding the hungry, caring for the sick, noticing the lonely, standing up for the oppressed, and loving the people the world forgets. It's extending the same mercy, grace, and radical kindness you've received from God to everyone He places in your path.

If you've never experienced this kind of community, don't wait for someone else to build it for you. Gather a few like-minded believers. Open your home, your table, your life. Pray together. Read Scripture together. Share your burdens and your joys. Listen for the Spirit's leading and look for ways to bless those around you. This is where and how the Ekklesia comes alive – not in programs or buildings, but in the simple, powerful, everyday acts of worship and service that flow from hearts fully surrendered to God.

This is what it means to be the Body. This is what it means to be His people. And this is what you were made for.

Chapter Eighteen

Living in Confidence

We've traveled a long road together in these pages, but in many ways, this is just the beginning. I want you to pause here, take a breath, and then remember why you picked up this book in the first place. It could be you were looking for answers, or were tired of the empty rituals; maybe you were hungry for something real, something deeper. Whatever led you here, know this: It was God Himself stirring your spirit, inviting you into the kind of relationship you were created to have with Him from the beginning.

We've seen how God's original design wasn't about religion, rule-keeping, or jumping through hoops to win His approval. You weren't created to perform for Him but to *walk with Him*. Sin broke that relationship, but Jesus made a way to restore it, not through layers of man-made tradition but through a New Covenant of grace, love, and direct connection with the Father, Son, and Holy Spirit.

So what does it look like to live in this relationship? How do you move from the page to the practice, from theory to reality? It starts with understanding that transformation isn't something you grind out through willpower or sheer determination. The fruit of the Spirit – love, joy, peace, patience, kindness, goodness, faithfulness, gentleness, self-control

(See **Galatians 5:22-23**) – these aren't virtues you squeeze out of yourself by trying harder. These things are the *evidence* of God's Spirit at work within you. You simply can't produce them on your own.

This is precisely where religion often gets it so wrong. It piles the burden on your shoulders – do more, be more, try harder – but true transformation comes only through surrender. The Holy Spirit renews your mind (**Romans 12:2**), gives you the mind of Christ (**1 Corinthians 2:16**), and divinely reshapes you from the inside out. The world sees the difference in you not because you've worked yourself into something new, but because you let God do the work in you, day after day.

It's a process.

Living a Spirit-led life is intentional. It's pausing in the middle of chaos to ask, "What are you saying, Lord?" It's seeking His guidance and trusting Him with decisions both big and small. It's letting His wisdom lead your steps, letting His love reshape your responses, and letting His voice become the most influential one in your life.

This isn't about you striving for perfection. It's about Him working and molding you to perfection. You'll still face trials. There will be moments of doubt, fear, frustration, and weariness. But in those moments, you will have *His* peace guarding your heart (**Philippians 4:7**), *His* wisdom lighting your path, and *His* love sustaining you through every valley and over every mountaintop.

(If you're thinking that's a lot of "*His's*," you're absolutely right. Think on that.)

This is what Jesus meant when He said He came to bring abundant life (**John 10:10**). Not an easy life. Not a life free from trouble. But a life of purpose, joy, and intimacy with the One who made you.

Stepping Forward Boldly

So, where do you go from here? You take what you've learned and you *live it*. As I've said repeatedly, the road ahead isn't one you walk alone. God is with you. His Spirit dwells within you. He has already equipped you with everything you need.

Cultivate that direct relationship with God: Again, talk to Him, listen for His Voice, search His Word, and trust the gentle nudges of His Spirit. Find or build a spiritual community where you can be real, where you can grow alongside others who are hungry for the same authentic, Spirit-led life. Live out your faith boldly and humbly, letting the fruit of the Spirit flow through you so that what you present to the world as a reflection of Christ is not the result of how you've changed yourself, but how God is transforming you.

To thrive in a direct relationship with your Heavenly Father is to align your heart and spirit with His. It's living in the freedom of the New Covenant, unburdened by guilt, shame, or the need to "perform" for His approval. It's cultivating a vibrant faith life that reflects His love and grace, not just in your personal walk but in your interactions with others.

Above all, trust the Holy Spirit. He is your Teacher, your Comforter, your Guide. Whether you're facing major life decisions or navigating the small, everyday moments, invite the Spirit into the process. He will lead you exactly where you need to go.

A Final Word and Prayer

Before you close this book, if nothing else, I want you to know this: You were created for intimacy with God; a direct, one-on-one relationship. The ache you feel for something deeper isn't random. It's the whisper of the

One who made you, calling you back to what He's always desired to have with you.

This journey isn't about deconstructing your faith and leaving it in rubble. It's about rediscovering your faith and grounding it in its truest form, unburdened by man-made rules and untethered from religious performance. Live with a faith that's fully aligned in God's grace so that you can step boldly into a life of joy, peace, and purpose, rooted in His unchanging love.

You don't have to earn it. You don't have to strive for it. All you have to do is say yes.

With that, here's my prayer and declaration over you:

"In the name of Jesus, I declare that you will walk in confidence, knowing you are held in the arms of your Heavenly Father. May you hear His voice clearly, feel His presence deeply, and trust His guidance completely. May your life become a testament to His love, not because you tried to fix yourself, but because He is transforming you from the inside out.

"In the name of Jesus, I declare that you will step into the freedom you were made for – free from guilt, free from fear, free from the weight of religion. Be filled with the Holy Spirit that He may guide you, and empower you to live boldly, authentically, and in the Kingdom authority God has given you.

"You were made for this. Embrace it fully. Live it fearlessly. And watch as God does immeasurably more in and through you than you ever thought possible."

Blessings to you. The next chapter of your story is written... God wrote it for you. All you need do is follow Him. And He is with you, every step of the way.

Epilogue

This book is written primarily for those people God has placed on my heart; the ones who've been frustrated, disillusioned, or hurt in the very place that was supposed to bring them closer to Him. Some have left their churches, others remain in quiet discontent, and many are still mad at God.

When you're frustrated or in pain, it's all too easy to overlook the fact that He wasn't the one who hurt you. Religion did. The truth is, most of us were discipled into religion: traditions, routines, and rules. But not into a direct relationship with God.

As a result, your faith may seem dry, disconnected, and exhausting. You don't know how to hear from God for yourself. You're feeling judged, burned out, or spiritually stuck. Not because you've lost faith in Him (at least not all of it), but because man-made religion got in the way.

If anything in these pages has stirred something in your heart – a desire to go deeper, to heal, to realign with God – I want to offer you some ways to take another step. This doesn't have to be the end of the conversation. It can be the beginning of a deeper walk with Him, one marked by freedom, clarity, and connection.

Wherever you find yourself, know that *God hasn't given up on you and still longs for a "real" relationship with you.* Even if you're angry with Him.

He's not offended by the way you feel. He's bigger and better than that. He wants to heal your heart. He wants to restore you. He wants to converse with you.

My mission is to develop educational resources and coaching pathways to support you and others who desire to walk in the relationship that we were created to have with Him; to help you move beyond limitations you've been taught (or have imposed on yourself) and into a life-changing intimacy with God.

I invite you to explore these opportunities. Perhaps some will resonate with where you want to journey next. You'll find more information on my personal website. Here's the short URL or QR code that will take you directly there:

https://dge4.me/resources

Author Resources

I welcome hearing from you.

Xavier LeMond

About the Author

Xavier LeMond is a writer, spiritual coach, and teacher who speaks directly to the hearts of believers wounded by institutional religion but still hungry for a deeper connection with God.

For much of his life, Xavier navigated the uneasy tension between traditional church culture and the transformational power of a direct, personal relationship with God. When he discovered how profoundly that relationship could heal, guide, and empower, free from the constraints of dogma and empty rituals, he realized that what had worked for him could offer hope to others, especially to those who had walked away disillusioned, discouraged, or simply unable to embrace what it truly means to follow Christ beyond the walls of religion.

Out of that desire, he developed the **EDGe Coaching framework** (Engaging Directly with God everyday), a Spirit-led model that helps others move beyond performance-based faith and into authentic intimacy with the Holy Spirit. He is also the host of *The Ekklesian* podcast and the author of several upcoming resources designed to help believers reconnect with their Kingdom identity, heal from spiritual trauma, and walk confidently in freedom and purpose.

As a coach, Xavier helps people nurture the kind of intimate, Spirit-filled relationship with God that becomes a source of wisdom, strength, and daily provision – straight from Heaven. He believes that bringing people into real resonance and dialogue with God is what transforms them into powerful conduits of His love and grace, capable of changing not only their lives, but the lives of those around them.

Through his writing, teaching, and coaching, Xavier equips others to live boldly, love deeply, and thrive in the unshakable freedom of the New Covenant.

He and his beloved wife, Rachelle, are both passionate about helping others discover that what they've been searching for has been within reach all along: freedom, deliverance, and direct intimacy with God, without barriers. The couple currently resides in Cedar Hill, Texas, but likes to spend their (scarce) spare time communing with the Lord in the Rocky Mountains of Colorado.

You can connect with Xavier, join this Book Reader's Private Community, or explore more resources at:

Private Community

If this book inspired your faith journey, please leave an honest review on GoodReads.com or Amazon.com.

www.ingramcontent.com/pod-product-compliance
Lightning Source LLC
Chambersburg PA
CBHW051518120626
46551CB00012B/984